Pornography
and
Masturbation
Addiction

Sacrifice

Trapped in the blue darkness scattered all over the sad World

My brothers

Take Love, don't get lost ...

Please read the all chapter then write a review

Table of contents

"If you gaze long into an abyss, the abyss also gazes into you"

Some darkness terrifies, some darkness attracts people. Bound by incomprehensible, insurmountable lust and curiosity. When the bewildered, enchanted seer stood on the shore, the abyss swallowed the abyss. Our book is about such a darkness. Blue Darkness, Pornography.

When we talk about pornography or erotica, we usually don't think about the dark. The connection between the matter and privacy, shame, forbidden pleasure or lust is clear. But dark? The reality is that we don't think much about pornography. Discussions about this are rare in the society. Need to discuss at all, even rare thoughts. Much of the talk about pornography is therefore limited to various levels of obscenity, suggestive humor, and ridicule. A large section of the society tries to avoid the issue completely. And a little bit of discussion, which is the objectification of women through porn; As a mere object, the presentation of women as meatpeeds comes up. But this is only a partial picture. We do not realize the true meaning of burning up of bad psychic imprints. The truth is that modern people still do not fully understand how harmful pornography is. But what has been known so far is enough to surprise.

Pornography is not an innocent pleasure. " Not a minor moral deviation. No such problem, the pretense of not seeing will go away. Pornography addiction is a serious threat to family and society. Because, its effect is not limited to the creation of temporary tension: in the long run. Pornography changes people. Intuitively, the human brain begins to flood with chemicals such as dopamine and oxytocin. Chemicals make us feel happy. The feeling of temporary pleasure creates a chemical flood every time you watch porn. The natural tendency of man is to return to that source which gives him pleasure. So dopamine-addicted people go back to porn. This creates a loop. The brain, accustomed to high levels of dopamine at one stage of repetition, may no longer be as happy as before. More dopamine is needed. More, more "hard" porn. Then more, then more. At some point the ability to rejoice naturally is almost completely lost.

If it is difficult to understand the matter, then read the above paragraph by putting heroin or cocaine instead of porn. It is the classic model of addiction. This is how every drug addiction creates dependence and addiction in people. The terrible thing is that in the case of pornography, the result of this addiction is a change in a person's sexual psychology, sexual desires and abilities. Just as a drug addict does not find happiness in normal life, a porn addict does not find satisfaction in normal sex. Pornography creates unrealistic expectations, dissatisfaction, and a thirst for imitation. Real is not enough for him. Unsatisfied with the search for happiness, he enters deeper and deeper into the blue dark hole.

Although started through the individual, its effects are not limited to the individual. Poisoning family and relationships. At one point, pornography began to have an impact on society and culture. The matter is already happening in the media. At one time porn mimicked mainstream story-movies. But now the mainstream media is imitating pornography. In many cases it is noticeable, but it is most visible in the case of recent Western pop music videos and Bollywood items. In addition, there is a lot of sexuality in the media and society as a whole. It is difficult at first to understand how terrible these things are for the individual, the family and the society, how wide its scope. Today you, me, our children, our friends, no one is safe from the poisonous scourge of pornography. Everyone is a potential victim. Millions of children and adolescents are trapped in pornography. Mutual trust is broken, countless families. Many holy spirits have been destroyed and the number is increasing. We are standing on the very edge of the dark hole. If our thoughts and attitudes toward the horrors of pornography have not yet changed, it is only a matter of time before an insurmountable dark society is swallowed up. So there is no chance to be silent, to be inactive. The truth, no matter how unpleasant or uncomfortable, must be revealed. Because, the price to be paid for silence is much, much higher.

So, stop pornography and happy Your Life....

How fast I grew up ...

A few days ago, a ten-year-old boy with curly hair wearing shorts used to sit under the kadai tree in his school grounds and look at the river bored. Waves that traveled far and wide in groups were crashing at his feet. Sometimes he tried unsuccessfully to count the waves. But he lost his temper a little later. Bored again, he looked towards the river. Never-or towards the sky. In the rainy afternoon sun, a golden-winged kite would occasionally fly. Suddenly he would call out in a sad tone. The boy would have become more bored.

Sometimes the boy would be surprised when he returned home from school, the sky was black and it was raining. The boy did not have an umbrella. So, to save the books from the rain, he would run with sandals in one hand and books in the other. Sometimes he would slip into the mud of the road. Returning home as a muddy ghost. Mother tried unsuccessfully to wipe her head with a bandage. Freeing himself from his mother's hand, the boy would run and jump into the pond. The raindrops on the water of the pond made a strange sound. The boy was surprised to hear the sound. After dapadapi in the pond for a long time, he returned with red eyes. Mother used to wipe her head with a bandage. Like a calm boy, he swallowed hot smoked rice in a goggle with a fry of putti fish, and the boy would lie down with a story book on his forehead.

It used to rain continuously on the tin rice. Outside, Sajane wanted the tree to fly away with the wind. The wind was blowing on the leaves of the banana tree. The boy would drown in the story book. Hakal Berry Finn escapes from the naughty father's clutches in a boat ... Can he escape safely? Or will his father catch him? Tension! Once upon a time a boy fell asleep. I was frightened by the sound of lightning. Mother used to come and lie beside me from time to time. As he slept, he hugged his mother's neck his closest man in the world ...

Still, the waves came crashing down from under the pot tree. Is anyone sitting under that pot tree counting the waves today? That lonely chilta Even today he may be crying. Still the sky is black and it is raining. It still rains on the tin rice. Does anyone hear the sound of rain?

Our generation is probably the last generation who got a taste of the classical childhood and adolescence of the abominable Bengal. Miraculous, innocent, humane. All the children in the same neighborhood are like brothers and sisters. Hoi-hallora, dapadapi in the pond, walking in the afternoon of Chaitra, amchuri, acharchuri, akhchuri, gollachut, fairy tales, our childhood was involved in a strange simplicity. When we say goodbye to childhood and reach the brink of adolescence, it is as if this civilization has started to decline at a supersonic pace. In fact, the decline began long ago, we realized then. This old world was filled with a strange darkness. The dish antenna brought down the curse from the sky, the stupidity of the stupid box growing in the drawing room. We have been pushed into the toxic temptation of high speed internet, smart phone, technology without any instruction. This new 'monster' is wrapped around the surface with a strong trunk like an octopus. We continue to lose the basic elements of childhood and adolescence; Playground, pond, river, uninterrupted leisure. The sky-scraping buildings penetrated the sky of our freedom. Land grabbers, factories, broiler farms, fish farmers took away our wetlands. The dilapidated state of the education system, the sick mentality of the parents took away our leisure. Where are we going? There is no place in the courtyard!

The life that was like the smell of grass flowers and motherly silver water, standing under the eternal constellation of Fagun, they were running after the grasshopper and the butterfly, the life that was Alif Laila and Sindabad, the life was to catch the statue The life that was lost in the playground of fairy tales, was full of complexity and instability. The undiscovered aspirations were discovered one by one, and technology came forward to fulfill those aspirations in a distorted way. We kept breaking. We got lost in the wrong current.

We have a lifelong friendship with one Akash Shravan. The bus was flying like a Pankhiraj horse over the chest of the wide highway wrapped in black pitch. I sat in the window seat. The curly hair of the head was flying in the wind. The bubbler trees by the side of the road, the dandelion flowers, the blue flowers of the unnamed wild vine, and the pool of the 11 kV electric line, everything was disappearing from sight in an instant. The silence inside the bus began to freeze. There was a lot of noise a little earlier. Sitting around me were several teenagers between the ages of fifteen and sixteen. Some were talking, some were bored and looking outside, some were sleeping with their heads on the seat or on his neck. The last boys are quite tired. A little while ago, in high volume, they were dancing to the tune of "Burkha Pada Mey Pagal Karechche" type song. I have never had the good fortune (or bad luck?) To watch such a dance. But on the National Geographic Channel I saw some of the jungles of the African deep forest dancing. These dances have a lot in common with that dance! Anyway the boys are my friends, we all went to the same class. From school we were going to picnic in Mujibnagar. It was an unbearably beautiful day in the spring.

The sergeants sat in the front seats. Just behind them sat a group of boys and girls. After getting off the bus, I heard from several people that these children had watched porn on their mobile phones all the way together in the bus! I was very surprised that day. Then slowly I lost the ability to be surprised to see so many such incidents.

I found out that my best friend at school was horribly addicted to porn.

The hard disk admission episode of the boy sitting next to me in college. The boy on the back bench

He watches porn on his mobile phone all night and sleeps in class. A close friend, too

Polite, shy boy, became very shameless due to porn-addiction. I saw

School friends are watching porn by closing the classroom door, college friends are on mobile

Leaving porn on the loudspeaker is annoying Madame, with Madame

Tiffin's time is passing with juicy talk. Ugly hints on Facebook

Making trolls. Imitating pornstars to new students at varsity ragging

Being forced to. The polite boy in the next room is also in the college bag

He walks around with a book of short stories, while the boy who goes to prayers is also with his roommate

Making fun of pornstars, will I be surprised then?

I had a big shock in the month of Ramadan 2011. I went to the village mosque on the night of the 27th of Ramadan. During the prayers, I noticed that some twelve- or thirteen-year-old boys were sitting under a mango tree in the outer courtyard of the mosque, watching porn on their mobile phones. Caught in the act, O God. In the month of Ramadan! On the night of the 27th of Ramadan. La hawla wala ku'ata illah billah!

At Darcy, I was able to persuade a few people to clean the hard disk. Some of them had hundreds of gigabytes of porn on their hard disks. When we grew up, mobile and internet were not easily available in Bangladesh.

That's when it was such a terrible situation!

Now think about what the situation might be!

The world is now a deeper, deeper disease. The uncivilized, polluted air like today may never have flown in the history of the world for hundreds of thousands of years. Leaving aside porn videos, TV commercials, billboards, magazines, movies, music, item songs, literature, poetry, everything is extremely sexual today. Everywhere only to make women products, to capitalize on women's bodies. Today, the sacred love of men and women is limited to physical intercourse with each other like an animal. Today, men no longer look for love in the eyes of women, they wrap love in the folds of women's bodies. Even heinous things like homosexuality and incest (na'uzubillah) fall into the category of human rights today. It is doubtful whether our previous generation will ever fully understand what teenagers and young people have to spend their days in such an unfavorable environment.

Our parents may never know, with hundreds of gigabytes of porn videos on their darling, innocent, polite boy's PC hard disk! Can parents at all believe that our children of this generation watch porn videos in groups? Physical before marriage Intimacy is a normal thing for them, group sex is also a very normal thing? The boy whose milk teeth have not been read at all is now familiar with words like oral sex, anal sex?

I grew up poisoned in the blue air at this time, the poisonous air has hit me again and again in my life. The ship was wrecked. Yet I turned around in the will of Allah (1). I dreamed anew, I looked through binoculars and found out what it means to survive. If we take a long look at childhood-adolescence-early youth, we can see that many pure human souls are drowning in the quicksand of pornography, masturbation and gossip without knowing it. Yet billions of pure Fitrat around are being wasted. Sometimes this society has a strong desire to turn this world upside down. How many times have I expressed my wish to the window of a moving train, the old golden-winged kite, and the neem tree in the courtyard corner. They smirked. My hand is clenched. I tore my hair in vain anger, soaked my eyes in a lonely afternoon at the pond in Bengali.

I could not do anything but look! Nothing!

I have a younger brother. This boy with curly hair is standing in the square of adolescence. When I looked at him, my past came in front of me in an instant, and a lot of fear came and surrounded me. Growing up, my little brother would have to face an even more intense battle in this digital age than I, my friends or a boy our age had to fight. Millions of my unnamed brothers are constantly fighting with this "monster". We didn't get much direction when we were growing up, but it was our small effort to keep my brothers from getting lost. There are tears and sweat of many brothers in this book. May Allah (d) reward them well, the graceful aspect of flying like a green bird in the flower garden of Firdaus.

We have cited various peer review journals for the analysis of scientific facts. In addition to journals, we have enlisted the help of various well-known electronic and print media for ancillary news including statistics. It took me a long time to finish the book because I was picky about references. Every effort has been made to keep it accurate. Even then it goes wrong There may be a possibility to go. Hopefully, readers will try to correct our mistakes with a forgiving look. You can keep an eye on this Facebook page and this website to get regular updates of our articles.

Drama, movies, media, stories, novels, etc. are very powerful means of controlling the human psyche. It is this media that decides who we will think about, how we will think, whose sorrow weep, whose joy we will rejoice in, what clothes we will wear, what food we will eat, everything. People walk the streets barefoot like Himu. Gives haircuts like footballers, loves like silver screen heroes, dresses like advertising models.

What the media highlights in front of people has a profound effect on them. You don't have to be a rocket scientist to understand that when a person watches porn videos regularly, his behavior will be affected by the scenes seen on the screen. But we do not want to understand why I know this simple word. Many times due to our ignorance, many times we just sit and claim to justify watching porn, "Watching porn is not harmful, I'm just watching, not doing anything", etc etc ...

Has porn-addiction broken the hearts of so many classical lovers, basic people and gentle women, how many tears have flowed from the eyes of a loving person like a bird's nest, how many colorful dreams have fallen because of this addiction, has anyone ever calculated it?

Child abuse, rape, incest, murder, human trafficking, drugs, AIDS, homosexuality, depression, suicide, divorce ... This is such a cruel world.

Inevitable loss

Many colors of clouds.

Sometimes as bright as blood.

Never blue.

Ever green.

Sometimes it is white like a flower. Now, of course, the color of the clouds is gray.

It's raining cats and dogs. Upset rain.

I don't remember if it rained that morning, but I know why I was so upset. I was scattering around the net sporadically. Suddenly I saw an article. Who knew this article would change the course of my life! The author has Munsiana, but through real facts, data and some scientific analysis, he is sitting on a surprising story. Porn-addiction is as harmful as cocaine or heroin addiction! I sighed. Although it took some time to digest. If you watch porn, the damage to your brain will be the same damage to cocaine, heroin, etc., you will be the same damage! Not only that, porn addiction will change the structure of your brain!

But why?

You don't play, you don't drink, you sit in a corner of the house and watch porn, yet why would you suffer a loss like cocaine or heroin use? Why would your brain be worn? - To get "why" he has to listen to some science. Trying to explain as simply as possible. A part of our brain is called the reward center (Reward

Center). Its job is to reward you, to make you feel happy, to motivate you to survive. 4, 5

I speak in simple Bengali. As a child, Feluda was addicted to reading. He used to say from home that if he got good result in the test, Feluda's book would be bought. After getting good results in the exam, I was rewarded for buying Feluda's book and getting good results, this is exactly what the Rewards Center does. The things that will move your life forward are eating something good, working hard to get something, the Rewards Center will motivate you to do those things and reward you at the end of the work.

But how does the Rewards Center reward us? What is the mechanism? The Rewards Center releases two chemicals, dopamine and oxytocin, for this award. When the Rewards Center felt something rewarding had happened, the two chemicals began to be produced at wholesale rates. And when these two chemicals are produced, the game is over ... just joy and happiness in the air in the sky. Joy, joy, joy. But sadly, this "reward center" is easily overpriced. Opium or cocaine stimulates the Rewards Center "comfortably" without any hassle. The brain begins to release dopamine and oxytocin. As a result, in the words of the poet, "Pain begins to be felt like happiness.

Like drugs, porn can easily flood the brain with dopamine and give viewers a momentary pleasure. ' Brain scans of porn-addicts and drug-addicts have shown that their brain structures are exactly the same. " But the rest of the picture is ... Hi

Dopamine flows through the brain pulse, creating new avenues for reward. As a result of the work that caused dopamine to be released for the first time, the brain wants to go back to it again and again in the lure of dopamine. That's why once you watch porn, you want to watch it again and again. " Only then did the milk teeth begin to fall out. I can lift the bat with great difficulty. A team was formed with a few youngsters like me in the vicinity, who had the ball but no bat. No one had the courage to give the bat to his father. One of them grabbed his elder brother's hands and feet and made a bat by scratching the branches of a palm tree. What a joy we have with that bat! It was a jumping game for a while, but then playing with this rhythmic bat no longer attracts the mind. In the meantime we have grown a bit. A beautiful bat made of neem wood was made by the carpenters. This blue bat is still floating in my eyes! How many sixes I hit with this bat! A few days later I lost interest in playing with this bat. A very expensive wooden ball playing bat was bought by raising money. The only purpose of such a mess is to make you realize that people can't be satisfied with anything for very long. This is how God created man. The same thing happens with porn. Suppose you saw a softcore porn. A certain level of dopamine releases, you get pleasure. Even if the same amount of dopamine is released after watching porn several times in a row, you will not get the same pleasure as before. You can no longer be satisfied with this porn video. You will need something new. Why is that?

When excessive dopamine is released, the brain becomes less sensitive to dopamine. That means the previous dose does not work anymore. This is because in order to protect itself from the effects of excess dopamine, the brain releases certain nerves whose function was to respond to dopamine stimuli. The function of these nerves, called the receptor nerve, is to receive dopamine molecules and send signals to the brain that I have received so much dopamine. When the number of receptor nerves decreases, the same amount of dopamine is released as before, but there is not enough receptor nerve to receive it, and therefore the amount of dopamine present in the brain is very low. That's why you enjoy watching the same porn videos less than before.

You just have to be more discriminating with the help you render toward other people. You will lean towards hardcore porn, it will increase the level of dopamine release and you will get the same pleasure as before. Starting with softcore porn to compete with dopamine levels you will gradually start to see heinous things like gay porn and child porn.

But this is exactly what happens to drug addicts. Starting that addiction from cigarettes

It ends up in cocaine and heroin. 12, 13 A very important part of our brain is the frontal lobe. What is the work of this Babaji? This frontal lobe is responsible for the dream of Abir in your eyes when a beautiful woman walks through the corridor of the lab. Our means of expression are language, decision-making ability, problem-solving skills, and above all, this frontal lobe plays an important role in controlling our personality.

Drug addiction, overeating, internet addiction, porn — this causes serious damage to the frontal lobe. The scary thing is that the more porn a person watches, the more damage to his brain and the harder it is to get back to normal. Because nerve cells are the cells in the body that never regenerate. " Although seemingly innocuous, I hope you understand what a porn video does to your brain.

The question is, "Before the eggs, not before the chickens?" Like the question. Do people masturbate because they can't control themselves after watching porn or do people watch porn to masturbate? Whatever it is, masturbation and porn are an integral part of each other.

I am writing this article with a huge grief.

It hurts when I see a group of people campaigning for masturbation: "What's wrong with religion? Science tells us it's good for the body." - How much more! In many western countries, school children are routinely encouraged to do this in the name of sex education. It is sad to see that in our country also some ignorant servants of Allah (1) with Muslim names are writing videos and making videos on Facebook and blog in support of this work. We will try to give an idea in this article, what seems to be a very harmless addiction to the seemingly innocuous masturbation addiction! At first we will hear the dark stories of some unfortunate brothers, whose addiction to masturbation has brought them to the brink of a deep abyss of destruction. Then we will discuss the horrors of masturbation in the eyes of science.

If we were not addicted to masturbation, our life would not be like that!

One.

I am speaking from Bangladesh. I have been addicted to masturbation for eight years. Tried a lot, but couldn't keep myself away from this dirty job. As a Muslim, it has always seemed to me that I have never invited them to Islam, but I know how much I know bad. I can't trust myself properly, my confidence is at zero. Suffering from inferiority complex all the time. Can't be easy in front of people. I used to have a lot of fun masturbating at first. I don't get it now. Just 20 seconds ... then it's all over. Many people like me a lot. To them I am a wonderful person. They only know my appearance; Honest, polite, faithful. If only they knew about my dark world! I am very dry, weak and forgetful. Occasionally I get sick. Friends give me a lot of "rot" with these. I am worried about the days ahead. There is always a fear of marriage. How will he come! Will he like me! Can I make her happy ...?

Tow

I was shocked that morning. I woke up and stood in front of the mirror with a lot of mind. I was surprised to see a 70 year old man looking at me. Seeing this state of mind, I became very upset. 31 I am in the midst of my youth, but the look of old age is clear on my face. I have big brothers. One is 39 and the other is 45. But nowadays any stranger makes me think of them as uncles! Of course I don't want to blame anyone for my condition. I am guilty. Have I not been addicted to destroying myself for the last 16 years? I started masturbating at the age of 14. I am now 31 years old. 18 years! 16 years to destroy yourself! One day it was all mine; Engineering degree, fat salary job, beautiful wife. Now I'm poor! I see very little in the eyes, there are a lot of mistakes in typing. Memory is absolutely diminished, nothing is remembered; Completely unproductive. He was fired from the office last year. The widow has also left. I wish him well. How much more me or could I make him happy! I'm finished. The will to live is dead.

You may not even realize what a masturbation addiction is doing to you, but when you realize you need to pull the reins of addiction, it will be too late. There is nothing to do. You fall on your feet, please save yourself from masturbation. Fire will do it yourself.

The new people of this old world have deep faith in science, sometimes more than faith in the Creator. In the arrogance of science and technology, people today try to blow away some of the words of the Creator. Again, even if it is not so 'violent', there is a feeling of contempt hidden in the corner of the mind of many. Many people do not want to accept the statement that "masturbation is forbidden in Islam". These ignorant people try to show how beneficial masturbation is for the body by cracking the theory of science!

In this article we will put masturbation under the burning glass of science. Let's see what science has to say about masturbation.

Masturbation will create various sexual complications

This one masturbation is enough to poison your sex life. And if pornography is added to it, then sohaga in gold. As well as holding hands, these two will ruin your life, the field of happy dreams that you have built with so much care will burn in an instant, just like the bitterness of Chaitra.

One of the causes of premature ejaculation is premature ejaculation. When masturbating you keep trying to reach the final moment as soon as possible, the top bliss is found. It doesn't feel good to be late, helpless annoyance comes and fills up. After masturbating for a while like this, your brain will understand very soon that you want to reach the final moment. He will then program himself in this way. In a short time you will get top happiness. Even during normal intimacy with your wife, your programmed brain will take you to the final moment in no time. Your wife will be dissatisfied. Masturbation will make you ineligible for sex. In the language of medical science, it is called erectile dysfunction (Erectile Dysfunction (ED)). , Will not be as hard as it needs to be, or will not last as long as it needs to be hard. As a result, you will lose the ability to have normal sex.

Masturbation will cause you to lose interest in normal sex. According to a 2015 study, married men lose interest in intimacy with their wives as a result of masturbation and watching porn. Intimacy with his wife is boring to them. " There is also a risk of developing a chronic disease called Chronic Penile Lymphedema due to masturbation. As a result, the penis becomes ugly

Marital unrest

Where normal sexual intercourse gives the gift of a happy marriage, a shower of heavenly bliss rains down on this dusty earth, masturbation, anal sex, oral sex adds the flavor of hell to married life. These perverted sexual practices are one of the influences of frustration, dissatisfaction, unrest and quarrels.

Cornell University Urology and Reproductive. Clinical Professor of Medicine. Harry Fish said of the harmful effects of masturbation, "Frequent masturbation will cause a person to suffer from erectile dysfunction. If she watches pornography along with masturbation, she will lose her ability to have sex one day. "

To reduce the amount of testosterone as a result of masturbation Can

First we need to know what is testosterone? What is the need for 28? Testosterone is a very necessary hormone for men. Simply put, it is the hormone that makes a man a man.

What are the roles of testosterone in human body? Let's see:

1) Energy

2) Memory

3) Attention

8) Self-esteem

(5) Self-control

6) Well-formed muscles

7) Physical strength

8) Ability to work

9) The seriousness of the tone of voice

(10) Peace of mind

11) Masculine behavior

12) Effective behavior

13) Production of red blood cells

14) Normal bone structure

15) To provide enough meat for sexual intercourse

16) To enable long-term sexual activity

18) Healthy metabolism production

17) Liver functions

19) Formation of well-formed prostate gland

What happens if the amount of testosterone in the body decreases?

1) Fatigue

2) Depression

3) Poor memory

4) Decreased attention

5) Excessive instability

6) Low physical ability

7) Decreased self-control

8) Decreased masculine behavior

9) Minimal feeling in behavior

10) Not being interested in normal sex

12) Decreased vision

13) Pain in the spine

14) Muscles are not well formed

15) Accumulation of body fat

16) Bone loss

16) Hair loss. 26

By masturbating you are eliminating this very important testosterone for the body. Alas! Alas! Now if you are in the mood for argument, you can say, "If masturbation lowers testosterone, will it also decrease because of normal sexual activity? So will people be excluded from normal sex? " In fact, there is a stark difference between masturbation and normal sexual activity. It's not just word of mouth, it's scientifically proven.

Our brains react completely differently during masturbation and normal sex. Because of normal sexual activity, testosterone in the body is not reduced, but vice versa. One of the reasons for the increase in the amount of testosterone in the body is normal sexual activity. In 1992, an experiment was performed on 4 pairs of couples.

To see what their testosterone levels are on the day of their normal marital sex and the day they have not had sex. It was found that the night after they had normal sex, the amount of testosterone in their body increased the next day. On the other hand, the night after they had no sex, the next day the amount of testosterone in their body did not increase.

In 2003, a study was conducted on the effect of stopping masturbation on the amount of testosterone in the body. The results show, masturbation From the first 1 to 5 days of abstinence, testosterone levels continue to rise normally. On the 6th and 7th day this growth rate becomes 148%! After 7 days, testosterone levels return to normal

Risk of prostate cancer

The number of patients with prostate cancer or prostate cancer is increasing day by day. Masturbation is mainly responsible for this. However, many of us are under the misconception that masturbation prevents prostate cancer. Well, let's leave out the debate and see what the results of the research are. Polixeni Dimitropulu (PhD), Rosalind Ellis (PhD, FRCP) and Kenneth R. Meyer (PhD) studied 640 people. They collected all the sexual information of these 640 people. Half of them were diagnosed with prostate cancer before the age of 60, and the other half did not. The results of their study were astonishing. "Normal sex does not affect the risk of prostate cancer, but masturbates. Between the ages of 20 and 30, masturbation increases the risk of prostate cancer. Compared to those who masturbate less than once a month, those who masturbate 2-6 times a week at this age have a 69% higher risk of developing prostate cancer at age 60. Again, those between the ages of 20 and 30 who stay away from masturbation have an 80% lower risk of developing prostate cancer. "Masturbation also increases women's risk of breast cancer."

Masturbation will weaken your muscles

The hormone testosterone is very important for well-built muscles. And if you gradually eliminate that hormone by masturbating, then yours .How will the body be well-organized? A man's body will be well-formed, beaten like steel, hard; Creeping like girls is soft, not flexible.

Masturbation will make you extremely inattentive

A 2001 study found that within 30 minutes of masturbating, the amount of noradrenaline in the body of the masturbator decreased significantly. What are the consequences of Noradrenaline deficiency in the body? Noradrenaline "is a hormone that plays the most important role in maintaining an uninterrupted focus on something. And that important hormone you are reducing by masturbating! Then how to stay focused!

Think about it, can you concentrate on the classroom table or any other activity on the day of masturbation, or are you always thinking uncontrollably? "

Masturbation destroys the effectiveness of dopamine

The importance of dopamine to us is discussed in the article entitled "The State of Drugs." Porn and masturbation upset the balance of dopamine. Decreases the efficiency of the receptor nerves, and even destroys the receptor nerves at some point. Dopamine imbalance creates many more new problems.

i) Depression

People's happiness comes mainly from dopamine. And when someone spends his dopamine behind the cheap pleasure he gets from this masturbation, he no longer likes anything other than his masturbation. Begins to suffer from depression. There are many ways to escape the frustration, anxiety, and mental stress of the workplace By masturbating. But after a while the frustration, anxiety, mental stress comes back again a hundred times stronger. 36

ii) You will become antisocial

If you upset the balance of dopamine by masturbating, you will always want to sit in the corner of a dark room and watch porn and masturbate. Meeting friends, chatting, going for walks in groups, these are bound to be annoying. The excitement of going to Mama's house for watching porn or masturbating is just milk.

iii) You will get less pleasure from small things in life

If you weaken or completely destroy the dopamine-releasing nerves by masturbating, and if your brain cannot determine the normal levels of dopamine, then the little things that a healthy normal person enjoys will not give you pleasure. For example, spending time with small children, playing cricket, getting wet in the rain, bathing in the moonlight on a moonlit night ... these tasks are up to you. Absolutely annoying, unnecessary nonsense.

iv) You will become effortless, lazy

The day started with a fresh feeling, the new sun and a cup of morning tea gave you the logistics to jump into the workplace with endless vitality. If you masturbate for any reason, then you will not want to do anything else. Will want to spend the day sleeping soundly.

Many of us may have heard the name of the hormone adrenaline.

It originates from the adrenal glands. Basically, when there is too much disturbance, the moon is released. This increases the lesson. The secretion of dopamine begins with the release of shadrenapine. After excess dopamine Excess adrenaline also starts to come out. Dopamine is synthesized to make noradrenaline, which is a hormone in our blood. Another stress hormone, cortisol, joins their forces. Together, these three increase our heart rate, extract glucose from energy-saving cells, and into skeletal muscle. Increases blood flow. And all this causes severe disturbance in our body. As a result, we often become restless, tired, or anxious. These are the things that happen because of masturbation. Not interested in doing anything new. The mind wants to sleep and spend the rest of the time. There is a pile of files on the table, the reading of the class keeps on accumulating, but he does not want to do anything

Masturbation destroys your self-confidence

Think of the situation right after masturbation. You masturbated and went to bed cold. In the damp air of the closed room, the questions of life, which you have not yet answered, began to float in groups. One by one, all the unaccounted events of life began to come. You started to get upset. "Damn! Damn it. My life was completely ruined, I am a Feltus, I am a Gandu, I can't do anything, I won't be hurt. "

To grow up, to be successful, confidence is a very important factor. Masturbation completely destroys your self-confidence. Stay away from masturbation for a month or two. You will see that your insides are full of confidence. In addition, masturbation also causes problems in controlling blood pressure. "

Why is masturbation presented as beneficial despite having so many harmful aspects? Why don't many specialist doctors find it harmful? We will have to wait a little longer to get the answer.

That time of the beginning of creation. Adam (6) was created. He lives in Paradise. Walk around feeling a little depressed alone. I repeat wandering in paradise in a bad mood. In the end, God created Eve (26) as Adam's companion. Adam's (4) depression disappeared.

Husband and wife and intimacy between them is a great blessing of Allah (1). They are soothing to each other's eyes, giving peace. Over the millennia, countless stories of this impossibly beautiful relationship between husband and wife, mutual respect, acceptance of sacrifice have been recorded, epics have been written, countless tearful anecdotes have been written. But in our so-called "modern great civilization" the relationship between husband and wife has changed. The relationship between husband and wife has become fragile. Formalin is mixed in love. Decreased responsibility and loyalty to each other.

Generations of our grandparents, grandparents; Not to go too far, it is difficult to find in our generation the amount of honesty and passion that existed in the relationship between husband and wife. Over the years, they have lived together under the same roof, endured all the hardships of life, fought against all adversity together, and stood hand in hand for life. The conjugal life of our generation is a lot like a picnic. Seeing each other, both of them seemed to have a lot of "kuwul", then they got married and "enjoyed" for a while. Then one night the two of them started arguing lightly about using mosquito nets. Then the quarrel. Then at midnight the parents of the two parties called for a divorce. Redemption.

After a while, seeing another person, I felt a lot of "kuuul". Then get married again. Enjoy for a while. Facebook timeline filled bedroom selfie, then one day hut divorced for little reason. This vicious cycle continues.

But why? Why is the sweet relationship between husband and wife, which has been going on for thousands of years, in its present state? Why the most turbulent times in the world One of the strongest bonds? There are many factors behind this. Capitalist thinking, forgetting the Creator, enslaving one's own instincts, spreading secularism, brainwashing the media, the rise of feminism ...

An important factor in this is pornography, item songs, the trend of portraying women as mere objects of sexual exploitation or "sex objects", and above all, widespread sexuality in the media. This is a serious but undiscussed issue

This article will be centered on us.

There is no way to deny that our generation has indulged in unbridled obscenity and arrogance. After spending an hour or two on the internet, they look at pictures of "when there is nothing to hide" type girls from different angles, it is doubtful whether our fathers have seen them all their lives. Thanks to high speed internet and Android phones, porn videos are as readily available today as potatoes. And our sons and daughters are swallowing it. An average of 26 157 people are watching porn every second.

Researchers at the University of Montreal have not found anyone who has never seen porn in their life. A study by security technology company Budefender found that 1 out of every 10 people who visit a porn site is under the age of ten. And these milk babies watch all kinds of heinous pornographic types of rape porn.

These boys and girls, who grew up reading porn videos and reading short stories, grew up with exaggerated, unrealistic ideas about sex. Pornography is also their medium of sex education.

According to a survey by the National Union of Students (NUS), schools

Eighty percent of college-university students are watching porn videos to learn about sex.

(According to Australian researchers Marie Crabbe and Dadio Corlett)

"Our culture has become such that porn is teaching teenagers, young people how to perceive sex and how to face it. Porn has become an effective means of sex education. "

If a person sees something over and over again and he likes it, sometimes he wants to see it for himself. So the trouble is starting after marriage. 4 Because of addiction to pornography, the husband has an exaggerated and unrealistic idea about the shape of the various parts of the woman's body before marriage. 45

His subconscious mind captures the bodies of all women like porn video actresses and real women are just as reckless as porn actresses in bed. But when he discovers the real truth, he becomes frustrated and the marital life begins to unravel.

Let's take a look at the back of the coin. Women who are addicted to porn videos also have exaggerated ideas about boys' bodies. After marriage, when she discovers that her husband's body is not like the one shown in the porn video, the husband is not able to act like the man shown in the porn video, or for so long, she begins to feel dissatisfied with her husband. The marital quarrel started. The beginning of alienation. There are Indian bastapacha serials to put a strong wind in the sails of foreigners. Neither of them is thinking about how much of what is being shown in porn videos is fabricated, how much is editing.

Call porn actresses "figures" and say different parts of porn actors, everything is presented in porn videos in a much larger size than usual through editing or they are made bigger by sweating a lot, by doing special exercises, by surgery.

It is normal that the bodies of ordinary men and women will not be like them. But viewers find it normal to watch porn. Thinking of her husband / wife special The limbs are small or unattractive. And a 30- to 40-minute porn video may have been shooting for a week, with actors performing sexually-enhancing drugs, while consumers watching porn videos in front of a blue screen thinking they've probably been in love for 40-50 minutes in a row. Can. The porn-addicted wife thinks, "If the actor in the porn video has been able to do this for so long, why can't my husband? Does he have a problem? " The porn-addicted husband thinks, "Hey, if he can do it for so long, why can't I? I must have a problem! " In this way, the husband who is addicted to porn is losing his self-confidence and the wives are also suffering from dissatisfaction. The love of husband and wife is ebbing.

Hundreds of studies by experts (sex therapists, psychologists, psychologists, professors) have shown that porn causes serious sexual problems. From erectile dysfunction to premature ejaculation, loss of interest in sex, dissatisfaction, loss of love between husband and wife, sexual aggression ... long list. At the present time, the sexual problems of the youth have increased as much as never before in the history of the world. According to a study written by 6 Navy doctors and many other experts, 14 to 35 percent of men suffer from erectile dysfunction. The number of men who have lost interest in sex is 18 to 36 per 100 people. Some of these men are 40 years of age or younger. Some are 25-year-olds, some are teenagers!

Studies conducted before the era of free online pornography have shown that only 25 percent of men aged 40 and under have erectile dysfunction. No one 35 years of age or younger would have heard of this problem. This means that in the last few years, the problem of erectile dysfunction among young people has increased by almost 1000%! Who is responsible for this?

1) 24 studies have shown that porn-addiction causes various sexual complications. When porn-addicts are confronted with sex in real life, they have trouble getting aroused or ready for successful sex.

2) More than 55 studies have shown that love between husband and wife decreases due to porn addiction. Couples suffer from dissatisfaction and dissatisfaction with sex life. 49

A recent study has shown that even young people are showing disinterest in sex! The study claims that pornography may be responsible for the sexual apathy of these young people. "

Young people in Japan are more interested in sex because of their excessive porn addiction

Absolutely lost. Young people in America have lost interest in marriage

Throwing. Porn addiction is one of the many reasons behind this

Expert ideas.

Porn-addiction changes the very idea of marriage. By presenting marriage only as a means of fulfilling desires. Marriage means not only the social recognition of physical intercourse, marriage means the union of two minds, a hand-to-hand fight for a beautiful world, fulfilling many responsibilities forgets this basic truth porn addiction.

Experts say that these young people are thinking: "I can satisfy my sexual desire only through internet porn. What is needed is the trouble of marriage Sharing the same bed under the same roof with another person, taking responsibility for another person. 653

Let's take a look at the adverse effects of porn addiction on sex life from the mouths of some experts. Former president of the Italian Society of Andrology and Sexual Medicine. Carlo Forresta said, "Internet porn is destroying the sexual ability of young people. It starts with a decrease in sensitivity to softcore porn, and the next step is a decrease in interest in sex. And finally the ejaculation stops. "

"Look, thirty years ago, when someone had a problem with erectile dysfunction, it was mainly due to old age. This problem usually occurs after the age of 40. With age, blood vessels constrict and make ejaculation difficult. It goes without saying that no one under the age of 35 could have heard of such a big problem. But that was before the advent of internet porn. Nowadays, online message boards are filled with complaints about the inability of young people to have sex. They suffer from erectile dysfunction not because they have genital problems, but because they have problems with the brain; That has changed under the influence of porn addiction. "

Cornell University's Urology and Reproductive Medicine Clinical Professor and one of the pioneers in the health of men, especially sexual dysfunction and treatment. Harry Fish said, "When I say porn is destroying America's sexual behavior, I'm not joking, I'm not exaggerating. I constantly see how deeply addictive porn addiction is in the relationship between men and women. I believe that porn is the only and the biggest unhealthy factor in creating tension in a relationship. It's hurting all sexual health. "

.... When a man watches porn and masturbates, he strikes himself with an ax. Excited by the on-screen scene, it gradually became impossible for Murray to get aroused by the real-world bloodthirsty women. He cannot be aroused or satisfied for as long as he needs to be aroused for successful sexual intercourse. "

- That's the calprit that will play twelve of your sex life. "

"Porn speaks of a virtual paradise filled with sex. Sex and sex, just sex. Different types of sex and infinite happiness. What porn doesn't say is that the deeper a person goes into that fantasy world, the more the reality becomes the opposite. As porn-addiction reduces the sexual appetite of addicts, it also keeps them away from sexual gratification. "54

We know of countless cases where a porn-addicted partner is not attracted to his partner, is having trouble getting aroused during normal sex, seems to be having sex, is not satisfied ', and is completely away from intimacy with his partner.

The porn-addicted partner becomes very picky about his partner's dress, appearance, figure, manners. He always compares his partner to the actresses on the blue screen. In manners, in speech, it is the partner. He does not hesitate to inform. This creates a pressure on the partner. As a result, they are taking the actresses of the screen as rivals and are entering an unequal competition with them. Haircuts, clothing, body shape, manners all have to change for the satisfaction of the husband or to attract the husband to himself. Anal sex and oral sex also have to say yes. But even then it is not possible to satisfy the husband. "

Wives think they are deprived, neglected, cheated. Growing frustration, growing depression. The characteristic of 71, 72 porn addiction is that the addicts gradually give up softcore porn and turn to hardcore porn.

"Light things" don't feel good anymore, something more "hard" to get excited

Is required. In real life, he wants to have sex in the way shown on the screen. Of the 63 most popular porn videos, 8 percent featured physical aggression and 49 percent featured verbal aggression. In 64% of the cases, the physical and verbal abuse is being carried out by the porn actresses who are being subjected to torture with smiles, absolute joy or silence. This means that the message is being given to the viewers that this is what women want from men, this is how women get satisfaction, this is how they have to have sex.

Men unknowingly abuse their partners during sex in the manner shown in porn; Verbally and physically. Can't even feel it. If his partner interferes, he rapes her, but he doesn't understand himself. Thinking that this is probably the way to intimacy, his partner enjoys all this. In the last few years, there has been a proliferation of heinous, perverted and forbidden sex, such as anal and oral sex. One of the reasons for this is the dominance of these perverted sex in porn videos.

The women of the screen participate in these perverted sex with a smile, so the men who are addicted to porn are assuming that their partners will also agree with a smile. Women are being forced into these perverted sex if they do not agree voluntarily. If necessary, they are also being beaten. . 1970

In porn videos, these sex acts are presented as attractive, satisfying, but in general, these sex acts are extremely harmful, unhealthy, dirty and extremely difficult for women. Anal sex can cause colon cancer in both men and women. Anal sex tops the list of sexually transmitted diseases. Numerous men are getting AIDS due to homosexual anal sex, and the number of women is not less. In addition to AIDS, it can cause serious diseases like herpes, gonorrhea, chlamydia, syphilis. 2

According to the World Health Organization, the germs of the deadly gonorrhea, which is resistant to antibiotics, are spreading around the world due to oral sex. Around 78 million people in the world are infected with this disease every year, which in many cases is leading to infertility. The World Health Organization (WHO) has analyzed data from at least six countries and found that gonorrhea is becoming more and more resistant to antibiotics. 3 Herpes, chlamydia, hepatitis and many more sexually transmitted infections (STIs Sexually Transmitted Infections) can be spread through oral sex. 64, 65, 6 Oral sex is one of the causes. 8 Cancer of the mouth and throat

Oral sex is one of the leading causes of throat cancer, according to a study published in The New England Journal of Medicine. A person who has had oral sex with less than five partners is twice as likely to develop throat cancer as someone who has never had oral sex. And those who have more than five partners have a 250% higher risk of developing throat cancer.

Actions like anal sex, oral sex reduce mutual respect and love between couples. These perverted sexual practices are one of the causes of marital strife, unrest, monogamy, dissatisfaction. Pornography anal sex an excellent basis for the social recognition of homosexuality by normalizing perversions such as sex, oral sex and bringing them into the mainstream of society. Making. Growing childishness. In Bangladesh too, anal sex and oral sex have taken the shape of silent epidemics. There are many such news on our page, even in the face of the wife's objection, the husband is forcing the wife into anal or oral sex. Porn-addiction cracks the mutual trust of husband and wife. Reduces mutual respect. A porn-addicted person cannot be satisfied with a partner. This addiction opens the door to everything from prostitution to prostitution.

Porn addiction creates reluctance to raise children. Raising children is no less a hassle! If you wet the bed at night, change the diapers, if you cry loudly, leave the happy sleep, stop the crying of the baby, take him to school, take him to coaching, how much more Hano Tano!

Porn-addicts fall into the trap of virtual sex fantasies all the time with porn videos. Absolutely irresponsible about real life.

Where is their time to think differently for the baby? Children in families whose parents are addicted to porn grow up in extreme neglect; Affection-love-rule doesn't get that much. Children suffer long-term emotional loss, fall behind in school, cannot easily mix with friends, the future becomes uncertain.

Everyone has a role model as a child. Everyone thinks that his parents are the best parents in the world, the smartest of them all, the one who knows everything, can do everything - Superman. Standing in front of the mirror with his father's spectacles in his eyes and pressing his coat on his small body, he thinks that one day he will be like his father. When boys and girls grow up, learn to understand the world around them, the depth of respect diminishes as the dark world of parents is exposed to them. It didn't take long for the ocean of love for parents to ebb in a small book. The daughter may feel a lack of holiness at the touch of her father's caress.

Sexual dysfunction problems starting with porn addiction, premature ejaculation, loss of sexual desire, dissatisfaction, sexual abuse, perverted sex, mutual trust, loss of respect, everything is bound to lead to a tragic outcome Takes; Separation. According to a study presented at the American Sociological Association, married couples who are porn-addicted are twice as likely to divorce. In the United States, 58 percent of divorces are due to marital pornography. 3

And many more problems start with this divorce.

Children in divorced families are more likely to be involved in criminal activities. Their incarceration rate is almost double that of children growing up in a normal family. Children from broken families are twice as likely to face poverty as children from normal families. At the same time in education or professional life they lag behind the children of normal families. They have different types of mental problems. Many are sexually harassed by their honest fathers. Many are forced to flee their homes অনেক many of them in prostitution, the porn industry, or the media. Many commit suicide because they cannot bear the physical and mental suffering.

It is a well-known fact that divorce robs people of happiness, frustration, and even suicide. However, divorce also causes financial loss. Married people with equal qualifications earn 10-40 percent more than divorcees. Every year across the United States, divorce costs people at least প্রায় 112 billion in additional taxes.

In fact, say porn videos, say Hollywood movies or Bollywood items — everywhere women have been made sex objects. The only identity of a woman is "sex". His arrival in the world is just to satisfy the sexual thirst of men. The man, on the other hand, is being portrayed as a muscleman, a sex power hard, sitting in the biceps triceps hat market. The sacred love of husband and wife has been limited In the middle of "sex". The ultimate goal and real purpose is to enjoy each other's bodies in a brutal way at any cost, to achieve momentary happiness.

The fact that love is not just a union of the body, but the union of the mind in love is a big lie today. For love, once a man wanted to tie a red cloth in the eyes of a bull, took a challenge to find 108 blue lotuses all over the world, wanted to spend the rest of his life holding his beloved in his arms, women promised to stay on the path for many years. Today those women, today those men are throwing the "love" in the dustbin.

Come out of the world of dirty fantasy in porn videos, don't be a little romantic by pushing consumerist thinking away! Learn to love and respect your wife like the Prophet (6). Forgive each other's limitations, faults and mistakes. Be tolerant of each other, be faithful.

He spent many long nights writing forgotten stories. Forget it unnecessarily

With the sunny, calm, unadulterated shores of love calling to the coast

In fact, the black cloud carrying the news of Rudra storm. How much more? What's more than Muthesht

Didn't? Now stop. How many more times will you be wasted in one life?

Fagun's Taravara One night, the two of them sit leaning on the moonlight. Remove the color of tears and keep an eye on her. Spend some time listening to the story of Hawa. Talk about rubbing salt in my wounds - d'oh!

"Girl, now I understand my mistake. I want to apologize. To stand up for life, to leave the filth behind, to return to that familiar shore of love. Don't you want to hold your hand like this in this adventurous journey of wish fulfillment? "

One:

Speaking of 2015. There are still a few days left for the rains to come. Disappointed with life, a very close brother confessed one day about his porn addiction. Details about how he has been masturbating by watching porn day after day since he was a child. He is suffering from sex fantasy with close relatives after reading short stories. I didn't even notice when I heard that a black cloud came over my heart and a heavy rain soaked my whole being. Only then did I start writing hobbies against pornography. I read books and write tuk-tuk. I had no idea how widespread the horrors of pornography, masturbation, and gossip were. The more the day went on, the more I struggled, the more I talked to people, the more I was amazed. Once I was surprised, my ability to be surprised was lost.

In front of my own eyes, I saw the "friend of life" of the school falling down injured in the clutches of pornography. Another brilliant friend of varsity life - a faculty of "comfort" could have been if he had been a little more serious - I have seen firsthand how porn, masturbation and cannabis addiction put an end to him. A few days ago, to talk about the porn and the female body of the children who had milk teeth.

It goes without saying that there has not been much research on porn addiction in Bangladesh. A 2012 survey of some eighth-grade students at several schools found that 8 percent had their own phone. The rest of the parents use the phone. Among them:

- 72 percent get a chance to watch porn on mobile.
- 72 percent watching porn in class.
- 6 percent spend an average of 6 hours on mobile.
- 43 percent use mobile for love purposes.

The most frightening thing is that as a private one, porn copies and music / ringtone filling shops on mobile phones are selling porn worth Rs 2.5 crore daily in the country.

In addition, the word "porn" has been searched more than 0.6 million times a month on Google from Bangladesh. The global number is 611 million times! The word "sex" has been searched 2.2 million times in Bangladesh. Has been done 500 million times worldwide. The same is true of other pornographic words. On July 30, 2013, Bangladesh News Agency (BSS) published a report on pornography. According to the report, the amount of porn that people of different ages download from cyber cafes in Dhaka every month is worth around Tk 3 crore.

According to a survey conducted by the Foundation for People, 6 percent of teenagers in the capital are addicted to porn videos.

UNDP Bangladesh and the Center for Man and Masculinity Studies

(CMSS) The school as part of the 'Braveman Campaign', a joint venture

Stage children and adolescents are addicted to pornography and ways to overcome it

A study was conducted to find out. The country has come up in this study

61.75 percent of school-going teenagers are addicted to pornography.

The study was conducted from April 2016 to May this year (2017).

11 to 15 years of schooling in Rangpur, Sirajganj, Pabna, Natore and Cox's Bazar

The results of the study were based on interviews with 100-year-old boys. CMMS chairman Syed Mohammad. Sheikh Imtiaz reports, "7.75% of school-going boys under the age of 18 use mobile phones. And 74.22 percent use mobile phones for the Internet. "

The study found that 61.75 percent of school-going boys view pornography and 50.75 percent of boys search the Internet for pornography.

According to the study, 63.45 percent of students addicted to pornography have seen pornography on their mobile phones for the first time.

Syed Sheikh Imtiaz also mentioned that 80.55 per cent of the school-going teenagers who watch pornography want to physically harass the girls. 12

Two:

No parent wants to believe their child can go down as much as watching porn. But the reality is big hard. According to research by security technology company Bindefender, 1 out of every 10 people who visit porn sites is under the age of ten. And these milk babies are watching all kinds of porn rapes. 13

La haula wala ku'ata illah billah!

According to a recent survey by NSPCC ChildLine, 10 percent of 12- to 13-year-olds are afraid that they have become addicted to porn. They think they can't stop watching porn even if they want to. Oh

A 2008 survey of 14-16 year olds found that more than one-third of teens viewed porn at least once a week.

The average age to get acquainted with a porn video for the first time is 11! The most addicted to porn are 12-16 year olds! ** There are many more statistics to be feared. If you write everything, it will become a huge book.

Will Gardner, CEO of Childnet, an NGO working to make the Internet safer for children, and a director of the UK Safer Internet Center, said: "It's hard for parents to believe that their children are watching porn. But the reality is, pornography is very readily available nowadays and children become acquainted with pornography at a very young age. 196

Three:

Porn-addiction has done the greatest harm to children and adolescents by changing attitudes towards sex. We will discuss this in detail. But before that, let's talk about other harmful aspects of child pornography.

Twelve of the academic results are due to porn addiction. 2015

From one study, researchers concluded that, "Teenagers watch porn

If they continue to grow, within six months they will have very bad results in the test

Begins to do.

In 2006, a group of German researchers found that porn addiction was a major obstacle to improving the academic performance of college students. Students who watch porn videos don't want to do much homework, skip classes, don't submit assignments properly. In fact, if someone is addicted to porn or masturbation, he has to spend a lot of time and energy behind it. After doing these Feels bad again. The inside of the heart becomes empty. Not willing to do any work. Sitting down, wanting to spend the day sleeping soundly.

While watching porn, there are some very strong chemical reactions in the brain (discussed in detail at the beginning of the book). When someone is addicted to it, all his attention is focused on it; I don't remember when the math exam will be held or when I will have to submit an assignment. It was not possible for him to concentrate on his studies. The scenes of porn videos keep turning in my head. She likes to be immersed in the fantasy of porn, it seems to study. Woodpecker, dull. The results were tested. Porn addiction gives rise to frustration and anxiety. Knowing the physical chemistry of men and women at a young age, innocence, Nirvana's childhood and adolescence are full of complications, frozen fatigue and mountains of grief. 19

At the age of mischief, of trampling on the field, watching porn in a dark room instilled in the minds of teenagers unnecessary fears about the outside world. She is worried about her future. During adolescence, the tendency to stay away from people works, and porn addiction increases it many times over. Adolescents become antisocial. He is ashamed to go in front of people, he runs away. Begins to suffer extreme loneliness. This frustration, restlessness, loneliness starts with drug addiction; Cigarettes, alcohol, marijuana, yaba, heroin, nothing is left out

Physical and mental development is severely hampered. Due to porn-addiction, he became addicted to masturbation from a very young age. Masturbation makes short life miserable. The combination of porn and masturbation gradually destroys the sexual ability of teenagers. However, the porn industry has committed an unforgivable crime by changing the definition of love. The media greatly affects teenagers. The media can easily control their life philosophy, beliefs, behaviors, emotions. Beliefs, behaviors, emotions of porn-addicted children and adolescents Needless to say, everything is controlled by the scenes seen on the screen. These children are exposed to pornography through pornography.

Because they have no idea about sex, they are the perverted sex of porn videos

Considers the ideal criteria of sex.

"Maybe that's how you have to be intimate with your partner, love is probably the same thing, that's how they understand when they love their partner, the partner doesn't want to be intimate, it means he really wants to impose a little pressure on me, you have to be a little rough." True intimacy, love, they do not understand that

Porn videos force children and adolescents to believe that women are just sex objects, coming into the world to satisfy the hunger of the male body. Women are also human beings, they also have minds, they have a pair of eyes, there is a sky inside those eyes, this reality destroys the power of perception, porn-addiction. The woman is like a piece of meat with which one can indulge recklessly, spend the night; But love cannot be lost, the stars of the eye cannot be lost, cannot be respected. The result of 104 is fatal!

There are porn actresses and movie heroines, the little brain starts to suffer in fantasy with all the women around with all its strength. Masturbation goes hand in hand. Sex fantasies continue with cousins, classmates, teachers, aunts next door, older sisters in the neighborhood, bhabi, aunts, aunts, uncles, aunts, even their own sisters! No one is left out.

Porn videos make children and teenagers forget that marriage is a prerequisite for sex. At a very young age they lose their sanctity. He wrapped himself in a sheet of filth. They grow up with a distorted notion of sex, which affects their own sexuality. Once you watch porn, you can no longer cool yourself by masturbating. Mete became sexually active at a very young age. Can't be satisfied with a partner, Frequent partner changes, some may be overnight partners. Rather than being bound by a trustworthy, selfless relationship, they become entangled in the complexities of "sexual interest". Imitates the scenes seen on the screen. If the partner does not agree, he insists. 105, 106

They have sex in all risky ways including anal sex, oral sex, group sex, they are infected with various sexually transmitted diseases due to various perverted sex without any preventive measures. Alcohol, marijuana and yaba go hand in hand with reckless sex. 106, 106

The more children and adolescents become addicted to porn, the more hardcore porn they watch and the more perverted they become. Anal sex, oral sex has been mentioned before, not to mention beating a partner during sex, strangling, slandering, forcing, group sex, even in many cases childishness, incest, bestiality ... and so on. No. 109, 110

Sexual violence is strongly encouraged in porn videos. Children and adolescents addicted to porn lose their sense of humor and become sexually abusive. He does not hesitate to rape. He wants to satisfy his lust with whoever he has at hand. A report published in Britain's Daily Mail has revealed how internet porn turns children and adolescents into rapists.

In England, the number of rapes by people under the age of 18 has doubled in just four years. According to the Ministry of Justice of the United Kingdom, 120 children have been charged in 2015! That is about 84 percent more than in 2011.

Justice Minister Philip Lee has expressed deep concern over the sexual abuse of children by children and blamed online porn for the decline. 11

According to the Australian Psychological Society, teenagers are responsible for 20 per cent of adult female rapes and 30-50 per cent of child sexual abuse. Professor Emeritus Frida Briggs, a child safety expert, claims, "Internet pornography is making a carbon copy of the sexual abuse of children. What they see on the screen, they are trying to do the same to other children. "112

Numerous incidents of children being sexually abused by other children, being "inspired" by porn videos, have been published in newspapers. For the readers we are mentioning a few facts.

1) A 12-year-old boy in England has raped his 8-year-old sister in imitation of a porn video. 193

2) Farzana, an 8-year-old girl from Sirajnagar area of Keraniganj, Dhaka, went missing on September 17, 2016. The next day, his body was found tied behind the house of his uncle Rahmat Ali. Who killed the innocent child?

Police started investigation. Earthworms come out to dig, not snakes, absolutely aquatic crocodiles! Farzana, a close relative of the child, was killed after being raped by a ninth-grade teenager, inspired by a mobile phone. He tried to deceive the police in a filmy manner. But the end is not saved.

3) Disoriented after watching porn, a 14-year-old boy abducted and raped a 10-year-old child. 195

4) A 15-year-old teen tied a 14-year-old girl to a chair and made a porn video continued to torture in imitation.

There are so many things happening around us all the time, we don't even notice. Very few of these horrific incidents come to light. The horrible thing is that porn-addicted children and teenagers can also engage in homosexuality. Anal sex, oral sex is a very normal thing for teenagers programmed by porn videos. To them it is normal sexual behavior. Unable to cope with the excitement of watching porn together with friends and the lack of intimacy with women, they often resort to homosexuality with their porn viewing partners.

Porn-addiction is also growing alarmingly among girls.

A study of 11,000 college students found that 52 percent had seen porn before they turned 14. 18 Another survey found that 1 in 3 women viewed porn at least once a week. According to one of the 116 most popular porn sites in the world, India is the fourth most viewed country in the world. And a quarter of the people from India who watch porn on this site are women. The most popular of these girls are lesbian (lesbian) and gay (lesbian) porn. The site was not referenced for good reason. This growing porn-addiction of girls is also changing their sexual perception. Day by day perverted sex, sexual-violence, rape them it is becoming normal. The tendency to engage in group sex is increasing among adolescents.

Four:

High school love! It is not clear when a boy who has just entered adolescence falls in love with a girl wearing a frock! The boy walks in the alleys around the girl's house with the coaching hoax. Maybe in a rare moment the girl will come to the balcony, her braided hair will float in the south wind. See you soon! That's all I want! This is the end of the boy's night's sleep! Bhuri Bhuri is wrong in the numbers, standing in the science class by ear!

The day goes on. The boy stays behind the girl like eighteen. One day the girl also likes the boy. The boy, who has just grown a goof line and unbuttoned his shirt, seems to be the most handsome man in the world. The girl bites the cap of the pen and bends it. Nothing sits on the reading table.

One day the two stood face to face.

Cosmic silence descends for a while.

Standing in front of the mirror, the words rehearsed hundreds of times turned upside down. The boy began to stammer. The throat becomes dry. Feels nervous. The girl immediately understood the miserable condition of the boy. Hanging a mysterious smile on the corner of her lips, the girl said in a hard voice, "Why is this boy so scared? Am I a tiger? Shall I eat? "

The boy becomes more nervous.

The girl flinched and laughed...

The complexity, instability, and other aspects of adolescent love are carefully presented in a very positive way, wrapped in a sheet of romanticism in a story-novel, movie-serial. First love, first Love, first come first served, and first touch ... all in all a complete package of bliss. The girls are presented as "queens". The boys are tenants, the boys are slaves. Adolescents, boys are going crazy to seduce young women, writing poems, composing songs, preparing to steal the moon in the distant sky. At last he is kneeling and expressing his love.

Adolescents, all the efforts of the youth, all the activities happening teenagers, centering on capturing the hearts of young women. Although it is possible to put dust in people's eyes for a long time, the real face of this love has come out in today's extreme sexual society. The stench is spreading in Pochegle. We have already discussed that porn addiction very quickly pushes children and adolescents towards sex in real life. And this puts a lot of pressure on the girls. Adolescents tend to pressure teenagers for intimacy. When they do not agree, juicy comments are made about the teenagers, satire and ridicule are made about the desire of the teenagers to be holy. 129 boyfriends play with girlfriend's passion. Emotionally blackmailed, "If you really love me, send me a picture of you topless." Topless picture technology continues to revolve around other boys' phones, unrestrained fantasy, and masturbation. Adolescents lose interest in maintaining a relationship if they refuse to go.

If girls don't send topless pictures or aren't interested in going to bed, other boys don't pay attention. In the end, the boys were forced to accept the offer. You have to give your body to the hungry boys. In the last 60 years, the age of losing virginity has come down from 19 to 18. According to Dolly Magazine, in 2011, 56% of adolescents gave up their bodies at the age of 13-15. According to an Australian study, girls have their first sexual experience between the ages of 11 and 18. The average age was around 14. " At the same time abortion is increasing. Countless children are constantly being placed in street dustbins and toilet commodes without a birth certificate. Being forced to accept any whim of her boyfriend in bed Girls: Be it perverted sex like anal sex, oral sex or group sex.

Anal sex and oral sex are very popular among teenagers for the sake of hardcore pornography. According to research published in the Journal of Adolescent Health, anal sex and oral sex are most prevalent among 16-17 year olds. In 1990, 1 in 10 adolescents experienced anal sex, but now 1 in 5 adolescents has experienced anal sex. Experts say pornography is responsible for the dramatic rise of anal sex.

Adolescents usually have a negative attitude towards anal or oral sex. It hurts a lot, I don't usually like it. But at the insistence of her boyfriend, she was forced into such sex.

A lot of times boys resort to tactics, "You agree, it won't hurt. Sure. "" Actually, I didn't want to do that, I forgot. "

Their thoughts have become such that, what is it that girls are in pain in anal sex? Maybe it's a little, but the boys are having fun, or the girls are a little hard for the partner, the pain.

The boys are boasting to other boys about anal sex, "I have done so many times

Have anal sex.

Trying to keep up with the demands of porn-addicted teenagers has ruined the lives of teenagers. Without bodies like on-screen porn actresses, they can't get to the boys; "You don't wear fancy clothes, your body is not like porn actresses. That means you are ugly, no one will look at you. " Helpless, they have started competing with porn actresses. Trying to be like porn actresses without eating, taking diet pills, having surgery.

In a little over a decade, 15-24 year olds have more than tripled their tendency to change the shape of their genitals through surgery. Adolescents are learning to hate their own bodies. Increasing plastic surgery, increasing the amount of breast swelling with silicone gel. 129

Adolescents are harmed physically by anal sex, oral sex

Being a victim. Rectal tissue is being torn, control over urination and defecation

Losing, even having to use their colostomy bags. Oral

Being infected with the HPV virus due to sex. Due to throat cancer

Many have to resort to surgery. 131

Adolescents suffer from anxiety, anxiety, frustration and depression. Drug use, suicide is on the rise. In just five years, the mental health problems of 11-13 year olds have multiplied, much to the surprise of experts at the Journal of Adolescents Health.

Depression, drug abuse and suicidal tendencies are also seen among young models, presenters and actresses in our country in recent times.

A 15-year-old girl was asked about her first intimacy, her experience. Innocently, he replied, "I think my partner enjoyed it. My body was exactly as he had hoped!

Think about the horrors of pornography! Porn videos have created a situation where teenagers do not have time to worry about their self-esteem and even happiness. Their main concern is to make their partner happy. In this porn-influenced, highly sexual society, teenagers are catching the main message of the society in a very short time: "You are a woman, you came into the world only to satisfy the physical hunger of men. He will use you as he pleases. You can't think about your own happiness, all your thoughts will revolve around giving physical happiness to your partner. "

Adolescents did not want too much, a sincere, caring husband; Whoever understands him, will embrace him with love, on whose shoulders one can rest one's head in absolute despair.

This sex-driven society, dreaming of their happiness, took them out of the house with fuel to fly the lantern of love. Tactically, he took off his clothes and served them in the open market, on men's plates. One sky made the temptation of freedom to make a male sex slave! Ever since boys began to see girls as "slaves" instead of partners, ever since this society made girls "sex slaves", girls have realized that her body is her wealth, her capital. The only tool to fight in this hostile environment. The girls began to use their bodies, becoming lascivious. As if the rotten boys can be rotated like a wheel in the fire of youth! Opportunities can be taken! The girls stood in front of the boys as rivals. The relationship that was supposed to be the sanctity of love, fidelity, cooperation, that relationship became rivalry, selfishness, deception, deception and transaction!

Five:

What is the condition of children and adolescents in Bangladesh? How deeply has pornography affected our society? Before discussing in detail Let me introduce you. Victor B. With Kline. Dr. Kline was an Emeritus Professor at the University of Utah. He studied at the University of California, Berkeley. PhD in Psychology. He also taught psychology. Dr. with the effect of pornography. Victor continued his lifelong research. Victor

B. According to Klein, there are several steps to take from the onset of porn-addiction to the final stage. The steps are:

(1) Addiction

2) Escalation Addiction

3) Desensitization - Decreased sensitivity

8) Acting Out - Implementing Fantasy. 135

Although Dr. Klein's model is "person-centered" to explain the stages of a person's porn addiction, yet we think it is possible to use this model to explain the overall impact of pornography on Bangladeshi society.

In the form of an epidemic, the addiction of teenagers in Bangladesh started several years ago. Before Smartphone's and the Internet became available, young people rented CDs to watch porn. From 2005 onwards, music listening and video watching devices like MP-4, MP Kiev started to become popular in Bangladesh. At that time, teenagers used to load porn on these devices with money from computer shops. But porn addiction has not yet reached the stage of epidemic. Multimedia phones became available around 2008. At the same time, porn addiction continues to grow. But there is no epidemic like now. 2010 Internet became available in 2011. Multimedia phones reach everyone's hands. At the same time, 'Item Song Culture' started in Bollywood. From this time onwards, porn-addiction became epidemic in the city-port, and village.

Dr. Klein's model reached the first stage of Bangladesh. Throughout this time, porn addicts have become mentally deranged, shameless and brazen Becoming accustomed to the behavior, at the same time the things seen in porn videos have gone to experiment in real life. That is. Klein has stepped into the third and fourth steps of the model.

2012-2014, at this time Dr. collectively crossed Bangladesh. Step 2 of Klein's model. Android phones and high speed internet have become quite convenient. The internet reaches everyone hand in hand. "Items continue to have an impact. Drama, movies tend to be more obscene, more sexually provocative.

Newspapers like Prothom Alo often publish news of a "special porn actress" of Indian descent. Pornography swept away children, teenagers, and young people. Kindergarten kids also find porn videos; The children of class three-four also became. Addicted to porn. Although many find it hard to believe, we have to tell these heartbreaking truths because we have enough information.

The process of desensitization began long ago. But pornography addiction has spread in the form of epidemics due to the easy availability of internet porn and Bollywood item songs (by definition items are also a kind of porn. Softcore, but porn.). Adolescents, adolescents, and society as a whole have seen an increase in sexual-psychological distortions and the tendency to accept pornography as normal (from 2014-2015 onwards). The more the playboy's image, the more "real men" he becomes. They are ridiculed, ridiculed, called eunuchs ...

The porn-influenced media and sex-driven society taught girls how to dress and move, so that you can keep up with the times. You will be the center of attention and attraction of men. Increased jeans, tops, t-shirts, tights and fierce make-up. Parents have closed their eyes and accepted the girls returning home after dusk, riding motorcycles with their boyfriends, make-outs in rickshaws and parks. ") Society has silently accepted the acidity of the roads. Accepted as normal. The mentality of the society has become so distorted, the bonds of morality have become so loose that the items are sitting in the drawing room with the whole family "Item Girl", "Porn stars" become the people of the house gone.

Bangladesh has now set foot. The fourth step in Klein's model: Acting Out. Implementation of fantasy. In the last few years, the inevitable consequences of porn videos, rape, have increased enormously. Children and teenagers are looking for Litton's flat and "room-date" at a young age. The pharmacy business has flourished, the bodies of newborns are being found in the dustbin almost every day. There is a growing tendency to video intimate moments, and blackmail is going on with this video. The video is spreading on the internet, the victims are hanging on the ceiling.

The method of sex has changed in a very short period of time. The amount of anal and oral sex is increasing at an alarming rate. Adolescents, young people are not hesitating to engage in oral sex in secret, in secret, even in the classroom or on the beach. Under the hood of the rickshaw, in the back seat of the local bus, there is the "Classical Louischami" in the light and dark of the restaurant novotheater and cinema hall. The widespread availability and use of the sexually stimulating drugYaba has had an impact on the overall sexual perversion of young people. The amount of masturbation addiction has broken all previous records. Increased sexual dysfunction, sexual dissatisfaction, sexual dissatisfaction. Adultery, adultery, prostitution, divorce have increased.

It is not impossible that the current number of porn-addicted people in Bangladesh has crossed crores. Plenty of new people said. Klein's model is stepping into the first, second, third step. Most people are probably in the third stage. Millions of people have become mentally deranged, distorted sexual thoughts are swirling in the heads of countless people. Given the opportunity and privacy, they can go to bed with anyone at any time, under any circumstances. When these people cross step number three and step number four, the blood freezes when you think about it.

From the close observation of the last three years, we would like to say that Bangladesh is standing on the threshold of a hell. Some people have opened the gates of hell with their own hands and jumped into the fire, countless people are waiting to jump. If the situation does not improve, if the resistance against porn addiction is not built, if the causes of re-addiction are not stopped, then in the next ten years the Bengali social system will collapse, the family structure Will break. Conventional values, noble customs, faith, respect, esteem, love will all take the path of extinction. Everything will go to the losers!

Pornography spreads its web like a poisonous spider. Anyone who is attracted to dazzling forbidden happiness and temporary excitement can fall into this trap. Once trapped, it is very difficult to break through the net. Just as a spider kills an insect, pornography will destroy you little by little. You will lose your health, your family, your job, even the person you love. In this article we will tell you some true stories.

The story of failure and humidity!

The story of sighs and silent cries!

The story of ruin!

Readers, welcome!

One.

Dad,

First of all, I love you so much and I forgive you for the loss of my life because of you. You should know what problems I have with watching your porn. You think it only affects you or you and Amma. You don't even realize how deeply it has put your children in crisis. I was 12 then. I just set foot in adolescence. That's when I discovered porn on your computer. At first I was very surprised. On the one hand, you have told me not to do this or that after watching Hollywood movies, and you have been swallowing all this rubbish day after day. What I see and what I don't see, when you came to say all this, I would listen with one ear and take it out with the other ear, because I knew you were a hypocrite! I knew mother was not the only woman you wanted. My eyes are also on the way you look at us Not avoided. Seeing you makes me very disgusted with men. Think about it, all men are probably perverted like you!

You tried to explain to me a lot, how my clothes can arouse the people around me and how I should make my own soul more beautiful. But in your work I realized, I can only be beautiful when I can be like the girl on the cover of the magazine or the porn girls you see. So I had no value in your words. On the contrary, I was very annoyed to hear these "lectures" of yours. As the days went by, this rotting society was just vaning to my ears, I could only think of myself as beautiful when I was like "them". Faith in you was falling to zero day by day, because it was the exact opposite of what you were saying. I have found someone who has fallen in love, who will not only love me for my physique, I will love the man.

When my girlfriends came home, I used to think, what are you looking at them with! As my girlfriend, or as part of your lost imagination? I married a man whose life was full of pornography. I have not yet been able to shake off my distrust of men. Yes Dad, watching your porn has had an impact on me year after year with my husband. I just want to tell you one thing, maybe you don't understand yet, your porn addiction has not only destroyed your life, it has sown the poisonous seeds of ruin in the lives of all of us. Whenever I think about how deeply ingrained this horrible intoxication is in our society, I feel sick. It feels so bad when I have to talk to my little boy about the horrors of porn. I mean, like the other ten evils, porn not only hurts itself, it hurts everyone around it. I have forgiven you. I am truly grateful for the way God has removed me from this evil influence, yet I sometimes get nervous. I pray that you may come out of this filthy intoxication, that countless more men may be freed from its corals. Your darling daughter.

TWO

Assalamu Alaikum brother,

May Allah bless your work. My name is Abu Sabbir. I am 19 years old. I live in Shantinagar. 36 Porn and masturbation addiction has poisoned my life. A couple of weeks ago, I found your Facebook page. I read several articles then. Many have shared their struggle against porn addiction. The stories of their struggles were very inspiring to me. I have been trying for a long time to overcome this addiction, but I can't. I am frustrated, tired, destitute, empty. Please help me a little. My story is a little different than the others. I hope you will take the time to read.

Let's start then?

I was five years old then. We rented a flat with two other families. The flat had three rooms but only one toilet. The family living in the left room of our room had a boy in class six. We used to play sports together, sometimes we would read to him. He was like my older brother. Hot, he started behaving strangely towards me. He would change his clothes in front of me and touch my body here and there. I could not find any explanation for his strange behavior. She would rub her hands on my sensitive areas and masturbate (which I realized much later). He used to say, "Look, you are my darling little brother. I will not tell anyone about this. "

Within a few days, she taught me how to masturbate. When none of our parents were at home, she would move her hands around me and masturbate. I thought it might be a fun game to play if my parents weren't home. I was a kid at the time. I did not understand anything. I could see that she was going to the bathroom and taking a bath after masturbating for a while. This went on for a year. Then they moved to another place. But in the meantime that is going to be a loss. Gone. By then I had learned to masturbate without him. At least a month I used to masturbate twice. I had no idea what I was doing, but it gave me lots of pleasure. Strange things happened at the age of ten. Until then, I was completely addicted to masturbation. One day after masturbating, I saw something coming out of my private parts. I was terrified. Acne started to appear on his face. The body became weak.

I had to struggle to pay attention to my studies. Then multimedia phones have just started to become popular in the country. A few of my friends had MP3 players. I started watching porn with them. During the tiffin period, before class, after class, I even watched porn while sitting in class. I always had juicy discussions with friends about girls. Not too old. But by then I had turned into a wild boar.

I got my own multimedia phone at the age of 14. The internet was not very readily available then. Still, I used to download porn as much as possible. School results continued to be very bad. Mental problems were already there, various physical problems also began to appear. I went to another school instead of school so that I could start studying again with a new initiative. But nothing happened. What will I study, I could not adapt to the new environment!

I was silent all the time, I didn't mix much with anyone. I would not even go near sports. Honestly, I didn't have the energy to play sports. Feeling tired all the time. I used to run away from school. I watched porn twice a week and masturbated. Two years passed like this. I still shudder at the thought of what happened at the age of 18. My real knowledge of the outside world at that time was absolutely zero; This was a faint idea of browsing the internet. Survival seemed unbearable to me. I couldn't do anything properly. I used to get angry with my parents. There were no siblings, no friends.

I wanted to blame someone for my miserable condition. But who should I blame? In the end, I blamed God for not finding anyone! All the fault of God! If he hadn't mixed me up with that boy as a child, I wouldn't have known about porn, masturbation, and my life wouldn't have been like that. I was never an atheist, but I blamed God. Then I thought I would associate with talented children. They may be my friends and I will get out of this hellish life and have a "restless" life.

I started mingling with the talented boys, stood on the street and started blowing bidis. Cannabis - or why not! I also started breathing in cannabis. Occasionally I would take some strong drugs. I used to paint the streets all day long. I thought maybe I have got the life of my dreams so far. But my porn addiction did not go away, but increased. I used to masturbate a lot as my body was bursting with energy due to taking drugs. A funny thing happened ... I fell in love! I used to watch porn and fantasize about "O". But I knew I would never get him. What madness I have done for him! Gets a smile now if you think about it. I cut his hand and wrote his name with blood, got involved in a fight, how much more! He talks a lot! Once the girl got married. I broke even more.

I stopped mixing with talented children. I stayed at home all the time. Occasionally I would go out just to buy cigarettes. The level of porn viewing increased further. Alhamdulillah! It was at this time that I began to learn a little about Islam through the Internet. I know it's a terrible mistake to do what I'm doing. I will have to pay the price for the mistake I made all my life. I also searched the internet for other religions for some time. But in the end I realized that what I was looking for was Islam, nothing else. I have already given up eating cannabis, this time I also gave up smoking. I started praying at home. But I could not give up my addiction to porn and masturbation.

The old Kasundi has been dealt with a lot, now let's talk about the current situation ...

I try to pray five times at home. I don't study, I live with my parents. No siblings, no friends. Suffering from loneliness, self-confidence at the bottom. Can't mix with people. Even when relatives come to my house, I run away.

I am mentally ill. It's kind of crazy. Talking to myself, people often look me in the eye. I don't remember anything. There is a severe headache, the head is torn in pain. I think I cut off his head.

Although I am 19 years old, people think that I am probably in my thirties. My hair is falling out, and I have some short beards, I don't know why they are turning red. I don't eat much, but I'm very fat. No matter what I do, I'm always tired ...

I don't know what to do. I became acquainted with masturbation at such a young age that my body reacts on its own. That means I masturbate almost every night. I can't stop myself even if I tie the trousers with the best. I sin unknowingly.

The strange thing is that after masturbating, I turn to pornography. Feeling guilty, I think God will not forgive me, then watch porn. I have a PC and a phone. I don't have porn on any device, if I get frustrated I go to Osbe's site. Sometimes I get

excited when I see pictures of women while browsing the web. Can't stay without clicking.

My relatives come to visit and are proud of the success of their children. The more frustrated I become, the more I go back to the realm of sin. When my parents scolded me, I became frustrated and sinned.

All in all I am drowning in a deep darkness. There is a hadith which says that on the Day of Judgment a group of people will stand before Allah (5) with mountainous virtues, but Allah (9) will crush those virtues, because these people exceeded the limits set by Allah (S) when they were alone and Allah () Disobeyed. 139

My Prophet () said about me in the hadith. When I'm alone, I do the same thing. Thanks for reading. Please help me.

Three.

My name is Amanda. I think my experience with pornography should be shared with others so that they can be careful. My boyfriend was a serious porn addict. From the beginning she started to explain to me that porn is actually a normal thing. Everyone sees it more or less. He also used to tell his friends that they also watch porn. Although it was difficult, I tried to adapt to his behavior from the beginning. But day by day it was going to an unbearable level. For a year and a half, I was tired of constantly fighting with my mind.

My boyfriend used to watch porn videos about 3 times a day. Her choice was rape porn (depiction of rape). Her thoughts were all about porn. Besides, he started torturing me physically. They tied me with ropes and raped me in various ways like in porn videos. They shot me in the head with a pistol and threatened to kill me. I could understand that he has mixed the fantasy world and reality of porn. What he saw on the screen, he tried to treat me the same. 140

Four

My name is Selina. I live in the USA. Porn videos weaken family ties, loosen the bonds of kinship, and sometimes break up. One day I hurriedly discovered that one of my uncles (he had made me a human being since childhood) was horribly addicted to porn. A few years ago I was at her house for a while to take care of her little baby. At that time one day I found a CD of a lot of porn videos in a drawer. The CDs were of such a disgusting category that even when I thought about it, my body became disgusted with hatred. Incest, rape, adolescence ...

Boo boo. What a horrible thing!

In an instant, all my faith and reverence for Uncle vanished like camphor. As well as the wonderful times I spent with him as a child, the memories put me in front of a big question. Wrestling with him, sitting on his lap watching TV — were these just pure affection, an expression of love, or something else ...? Since I don't have the right answer, I can't trust him anymore. I feel uncomfortable if my daughter is around her

I would like to say to the porn addicts, "Would you be happy if any of your close relatives saw you watching incest porn? How do you feel?

One of the strange darkness!

Speaking of the first year of varsity. I am returning home after spending the holiday at home. Night journey alone, so everyone in the house is quite tense. Phone after phone was making him restless. No one could sleep in anxiety.

The train left much after 11 pm. My mother fell asleep long before 11 o'clock, but she was awake that day. I called my mother, she fell asleep after my phone call. "Brother, can you make a call from your phone?"

I turned to the questioner sitting in the side seat. Age like 24/25 years.

The lower class. Surprised, I said in an annoyed tone, "Yes, you do."

My annoyance was easily felt. He said in an apologetic tone, "Brother lost my phone yesterday. The old mother is thinking at home. If I don't call, my mother won't be able to sleep. " Called her next door from my phone (her mother doesn't have a phone either). He told his mother that he had got on the train well.

The mother who sleeps on a comfortable bed in the AC room has the same worries for her child as the mother who sleeps on the sidewalk has the same worries for her child. There is nothing wrong with this love of mothers towards their children, there is no adulteration. A large part of our young generation is repaying this unearthly love of mothers, sister's affection by reading short stories written about them! We have made the online world so sick that typing in Bengali and searching for something on Google is scary, a healthy person is prone to it.

A huge generation has emerged and is emerging who are getting acquainted with the world of extreme pornography before they cross the boundaries of primary school. Those who read gossip filled with myths about their mothers, sisters, kamin, bhabi, aunts, aunts and uncles and suffer in sex fantasies day and night. Just as some people claim that I am not just watching porn to justify watching porn, there is no shortage of people arguing for gossip.

Is that really it? Chatigalpa is not harmful? Chatigalpa, just like porn videos

It can have a terrible effect on the reader. Books, words, writing are a very powerful medium to influence the human psyche. We can look at the Qur'an. This holy book containing the word of Allah is in the hearts of millions of people

The direction has changed and is doing. Hard-hearted people than stone

Reading the Qur'an cries like a child, reading this Qur'an is for Allah

People do not hesitate to give up their lives.

There is no way to underestimate the impact of the book. While reading short stories, the reader gets time to think about the issues for a long time. If he wants to, he stops reading and drowns in sex fantasy. But in the case of porn videos the scope is limited. The scene changes rapidly, there is not much time to think. Reading a book on a subject is more important than watching a video or listening to a lecture. The things read in the chat gossip sit in the reader's mind for a long time. The events of the story keep chirping like worms in my head all the time. Distorted disobedient thoughts are not easy to get rid of.

And if you keep distorted thoughts in your head all the time, it will affect your behavior. It acts as a trigger for watching porn or masturbating. The intoxication of chatigalpa will one day push you towards masturbation and porn addiction. Usually, people enter this obscene, vulgar, horrible world with the intoxication of gossip, climb the fence of masturbation, porn-addiction and go to Lytton's flat; Maybe I made a mistake, not in Lytton's flat, the path ends in the pit of hell fire.

If you've ever been in the trap of this heinous drug, think of the following. When you first started reading short stories, when you read the stories written about mother, sister, aunt, sister-in-law, aunt, uncle, cousin, aunt next door, teacher, working girls, you would not have thought, how horrible are the stories? But gradually that became normal for you. You started to fantasize about them, you started to pay for their different behaviors, you started to see them in the eyes of foxes. Tactful to subdue, maybe looking for an opportunity, right? Do not deny.

Naturally, the thinking of Bengali boys is a little different with some close relatives (bhabi, shali, kazin). Chatigalpa presents them in the way they want, using Rangchang in their disobedient thoughts.

The main problem of chatigalpa is here. It will give you a lot of false information about sex and at some point you will take it for granted. Really maybe they want something from me, interested in going to bed with me ... etc, etc. Your thoughts will not stop here, try to apply the techniques of female hunting in your life. Have you ever wondered what would happen if you read the stories of perverted thoughts and erupt the "work" volcano that is constantly building inside you? How many houses will be broken, relationships and lives will be ruined? Think about your parents. What a shame, they will be humiliated!

The intoxication of chatigalpa will destroy you to the core. Your eyesight will decrease, your memory will decrease. There will be a big change in your brain and this change is harmful. Michigan State University conducted an experiment on how chat stories change women's attitudes about sex. It was found that women who read gossip are more likely to drink alcohol. They have more than one sexual partner, they have free sex, they are obsessed with arrogance. 143

Allah () says, "Do not go near adultery. Surely it is obscenity

Misguidance "

(Surat al-Isra: 17:32)

But God did not say, do not commit adultery. He said, do not go to adultery - stay away from everything that can lead you to adultery. Whether the habit of reading short stories will lead you to adultery is a matter of discussion later, the real point is that reading short stories includes adultery.

The Prophet (peace and blessings of Allaah be upon him) said,

"He will get the part of adultery that is written on the children of Adam. The zina of the eyes is to look at forbidden things, the zina of the two ears is to listen, the zina of the tongue is to talk, the zina of the hands is to touch, the zina of the feet is to walk, the zina of the heart is to desire and desire. "

(Sahih Muslim: 6925; Sunanul Baihaqi: 13693)

Then calculate how many types of adultery you have committed. First of all, he searched by pressing the keyboard with his hand, took out a chat story and committed adultery with his hand. Secondly, Zina saw the forbidden thing with her own eyes and read it. Thirdly, he thought about the things he had read in his heart and thought, "Ish! If only it was like this once! "

Now listen to another hadith. Very scary hadith.

The Prophet (peace and blessings of Allaah be upon him) said, "I saw in a dream a stove with the upper part pressed and the lower part wide and the fire was heating up there. This situation was going on.

I asked Jibril (B), "Who are these? Gabriel (B) said, "These are the adulterers, men and women. **

(Sahih Bukhari: 136)

The fires of hell are so terrible that if there is not a second, a microsecond or even less time, then he will forget all the joys, all the fun, all the comforts of the world. Maybe he was the happiest person in the world, he never faced any hardships in his life, he stayed in the king's house, ate whatever he wanted, drank as much as he wanted. But one moment of hell is enough to make you forget all the happy memories of the world. He is having temporary fun reading short stories but is slowly building a huge mountain of sin. And the fire of hell is being heated for your entertainment. Save yourself! Save me from the fire of hell! There is no way that the fire can not be tolerated!

On the other side of the screen

After a while, the animal inside started moaning. Can't suppress in any way. At one point he left everything and ran to the PC. Connect to the net and log in to your preferred X-rated website. Browsing page after page like crazy. You are watching the pictures and videos of porn actresses on every page, constantly swallowing. In the world of fantasy, every body is eating with gusto.

At that time, a picture of a porn actress took you to the extreme of excitement. Burned and destroyed in the fire of work. You want the taste of his body. With great difficulty you removed your eyes from the grooves of your body, looked at her face and sat down to discover - this is your sister!

Think about how you feel at that moment! My brother, the women on the other side of the blue screen are also someone's sister, someone's daughter. They also had a family, their parents caressed them, Maya-Mamta was naughty with their younger brother, they also had a sea of love for their loved one. There was quarreling, eavesdropping, arrogance. But suddenly their lives changed in a gust of wind. Have you ever wanted to know the stories on the other side of the screen?

One picture, one video is stuck in the heart of one of your sisters, one of your brothers. Behind the scenes of celluloid, we may not be able to understand all the cries and nightmares of the unfortunate actors and actresses of porn videos trapped in the four concrete walls. But even then, what's wrong with trying to tell the story of this unseen world? Let's get back to that hell called porn industry.

Confessions of former porn actresses

"... Like all other porn actresses, I always lie. Me

When people ask, how did you feel when you did that hardcore sinta of that video? I smiled and said, "If I didn't like it, would I do that? I don't do any work if I don't like it, I have full freedom to work in the porn industry. " That's how I have to lie day after day. The real truth is me

I never want to act in these scenes. But if you don't act in those scenes

I will never get a job in this industry. "

"Even with a fever of 104 degrees, I had to shoot for hours. I was crying. I really wanted to go home. But my agent didn't want me to leave the shooting unfinished and go home. Being helpless, I had to work with a very bad body. "

"... (in the porn industry) I started with gang rape videos. Mr. with five people. The trainer raped me. This incident turned the corner of my life. He threatened to shoot me if I did not do this. I have never experienced anal sex before. This work tore me apart. They treated me like a plastic doll filled with air; I was thrown into the air randomly. I used to play musical chairs with all the parts of my body. I have never been so scared, never so humiliated and insulted in my life. "

"... I had to take emergency treatment more than 10 times for various physical, sexual and bacterial illnesses, yet I did not give up pornography because these are very common occurrences in the porn industry. I have seen many girls with chlamydia, gonorrhea and other sexually transmitted diseases (STD Sexually Transmitted Disease). They consider these incurable and contagious diseases to be very normal. "

"... I have worked in scenes where I have had to let others rape me by playing dead people. Home with bruises on the body.

There would have been bleeding if you had worked in a more violent scene. During the shooting, they slapped me, spat on me, and insulted me. I used to vomit anymore I just had to keep shooting ... I had a runny nose, I couldn't breathe! "

"... Honestly I hate my life. I hate myself a lot too. I don't want to survive. I have tried to commit suicide several times. ",

Torture

Rough and painful sex scenes including slapping, inhuman torture, spitting are popular in the porn industry these days. Even male actors squeeze the actress's face inside the commode of the toilet after sex and pull the flash. This is the climax in this industry! The best-selling 8% porn video is full of horrific physical and mental abuse

High mortality

Between 2003 and 2014 in San Fernando Valley, California

Of the 1,500 sex workers in the local porn industry, 226 have died. Them

The cause of death? AIDS, suicide, and drug use. Many have been killed. No other industry in the world — even the music industry, which is 10 times larger than the porn industry এবং and where occasional suicides occur is not so terrible. Where the average life expectancy of an average American is 7.6 years, the life expectancy of a porn actor or actress is only 36.2 years.

Sexually Transmitted Diseases

According to the Los Angeles Department of Health, porn actors or actresses are 10 times more likely to be infected with chlamydia and gonorrhea than the average person aged 20-24. The risk of contracting these diseases among pornstars is unimaginably high. A female doctor, who is also a former porn actress and founder of AIM (Adult Industry Medical Healthcare Foundation), has acknowledged the prevalence of sexually transmitted diseases in the porn industry.

He added, "6% of sex workers suffer from herpes, 12-26% from STD, and 8% from HIV." Testing for sexually transmitted diseases is not covered by the Pornography Act. Employees have to be tested at their own expense. 149

High Rate of Drug Addiction

Performing in perverted sex scenes in porn videos puts a lot of stress on the actors and actresses. The inside is hollow, clumsy.Embracing great exhaustion and depression all around. To forget the filth of life, they grab a bottle of wine. Cannabis, heroin, cocaine, crystal meth — nothing is left out. Apart from that, it is not possible to act in some special scenes of porn videos without being addicted to drugs. "The drugs we use the most are ecstasy, cocaine, marijuana, xanax, valium, vicadine and alcohol," said one porn actress.

A 2012 survey of 18 porn actresses found that 69% of porn actresses had used marijuana at least once in their lives, 39% had used hallucinogens, 50% had used ecstasy, 44% had used cocaine at least once, crystalmeth or methamphetamine 26% of actresses have used different types of tantrums. 26% and 10% of actresses have used heroin. 161

In January 2008, a male porn actor wrote on his blog, "Drugs are a big problem in our industry. If someone tells you something else, he does. Lying. Countless girls have lost all desire to survive just because of this drug. It is very difficult to think of this reality and their decline is very painful, at least to me. Admittedly, most drug addicts cannot get out of their cursed life without professional help. I have seen arbitrary use of drugs from shooting sets to parties, even cars.

Approximately 90% of the porn industry's manpower (performers, drivers, agents, owners, etc.) is addicted to marijuana. The girl who was "acting" with me on the set a few days ago suddenly fainted. He was addicted to oxycontin. Another girl overdoses on GHB (GHB-party drug that does not mix easily with alcohol). There are cases where a girl has received a "Prestigious Award" for acting in porn but she was so intoxicated that she could not even go to fetch the award.

The question is why drugs are so readily available here? First, there are mainly 18- to 21-year-old girls, many of whom are uneducated or poorly educated. There are many who came to say that they were previously penniless or worked cheaply in their father's shop.

Here they earn 10 thousand dollars a month. If you work for 5 hours for 10-12 days in a month. Drug dealers prey on them like sharks. These girls have a lot of leisure time and raw money. It is not wrong for drug dealers to make bets in pairs. 152

Many of us think that the work of porn actors is probably the most fun work in the world. They are having fun and getting money again! The idea is wrong. Porn actors have to take a lot of sexual stimulants to act. As a result, they suffer from various complex diseases. With exhaustion, frustration, guilt So there it is. He became addicted to drugs. Most of the money he earns from acting in porn videos goes to drugs. Their attitude towards women changed completely. They cannot love any woman. What is love, it is forgotten. How can a man be complete without a woman? From the beginning of creation to the end, men are indebted to women. By bathing in women's water, men have become pure, civilized and holy.

Men have got the courage to walk in the path of life's friend not because women have held hands in the way of life's friend. Porn actors can't fall in love with any woman, what a tragic outcome in life! What a terrible insult to masculinity.

Human Trafficking

Why do people come to work in this terrible industry? There are several factors behind this. Teenagers, ignorant of the realities of the world, are dazzled by the glamor of the porn industry. They set foot in this dark world with colorful dreams of fame, money, reckless sex life. Cheating in love, rape, child sexual abuse, parental divorce are also among the reasons. Many come to work in the industry out of tuition fees, drug money or unemployment frustrations. However, a large number of porn actresses enter the industry and fall prey to human traffickers.

After the drug trade, human trafficking is the largest and most well-organized industry in the modern civilized world. The human trafficking business is worth about 150 billion Dollar annually.

Women and children are trafficked in America just to meet the needs of the sex industries. To better understand the horrors of human trafficking to meet the demands of the sex trade, we need to know some facts:

According to Arnie Allen, president of the National Center for Missing and Exploited Children, the sex industry (prostitution, porn) is unique to the United States.

About one lakh children are trafficked every year for indices. * According to Steve Wagner, former director of the US Department of Health and Human Services Human Trafficking Program, that number is about 1.5 million. 156

Every year, six to eight lakh women and children are trafficked all over the world. Most of them are in the European-American sex industries (brothels, porn industry, strip clubs, etc.).

The way pornography is creating demand for Adam traders

American Shared Hope International once produced a report on the factors that affect sex trafficking. The report found that the porn industry was one of the factors that led to some inhumane human trafficking (most of which involved women and children). Or as sex slaves in the porn industry. Sometimes women and children are trafficked just to meet the demands of the porn industry. But why is human trafficking involved with the porn industry?

You will find the answer to this question in the midst of how pornography changes one's brain. According to scientists, our brain has a kind of brain cell called "mirror nerve". These nerves are stimulated when we do something ourselves or see what others are doing. This is why the scenes in the film make us cry or get scared. This is why some people are intense when watching football games on tv a mixture of excitement and emotion is involved in the game. Think about it, don't you think the star footballer's foot magic on the playground, Ish! If I could play like them! Call them footballers, call them heroes of movies or serials, but you subconsciously imitate them even if you don't want to - starting from clothes, attitudes, conversations, walks, haircuts ... isn't it?

When a person watches porn videos for hours, becomes addicted to pornography, he also wants to apply the things seen on the screen in real life. We have already discussed this in detail. And for the generation that has sex education, the only or the main means of getting an idea about sex, pornography, for the generation that has been involved in pornography since childhood, sex means the same thing - sex seen in porn videos. But these porn videos are a false, distorted and exaggerated story in the name of sex.

Sex is being presented in such a way that it is impossible for a healthy normal person to even think about it. Although most people now view pornography as normal. And at the same time there is a terrible oppression on women. When a porn-addict goes to the reality of what he sees on screen, he has to face a number of problems.

First, as mentioned earlier, adolescents are exposed to pornography at a very young age, leading them to engage in real sex. If they can't meet their physical needs through marriage or girlfriend boyfriend, they are forced to go to prostitution. Thus the demand for prostitution increases, human trafficking increases.

Second, the companions of porn-addicts can't be as rude as the porn actresses in the bedroom in most cases. Do not want to imitate the scenes shown in porn videos. But a person who is addicted to porn is in a situation where he cannot be satisfied in any way if he cannot do the sexual behaviors seen in porn. Once he was forced to go to a brothel. Prostitutes turn to human traffickers to meet the needs of their clients, and millions of helpless women and children fall prey to human traffickers.

Those who watch porn videos may find it hard to believe. But there are thousands of porn addicts whose end result was going to prostitution. A survey of 654 prostitutes in nine countries found that Forty-eight percent of prostitutes say their clients force them to do exactly what they have seen in porn videos before. According to the 181 Oral History Project survey, 8% of prostitutes say that their clients show their porn videos and that they imitate the actress on screen.

Laura Lederer, a senior adviser to the US State Department on human trafficking, has said bluntly that pornography is a marketing tool for commercial sex trafficking. 163

Third, porn-addicts seek out physical beauty in their mates like porn actresses. I always compare the bodies of porn actresses with the bodies of their partners. But they have to be frustrated. Porn actresses bring artificial beauty to their bodies in a variety of other ways, including surgery, which is not common among normal people. So porn addicts go to prostitutes who have bodies like porn actresses instead of their partner's "pansy" body. And human trafficking is done to provide prostitution.

Fourth, the victims of human trafficking are forcibly used in porn videos. Especially in hardcore pornography. Sixty percent of victims of human trafficking say they have been forced to participate in porn videos. 18 New slavery is going on around pornography. Women victims of human trafficking are being made sex slaves. But "Islam makes women sex slaves" The screaming Western world and their ideological children, the brown-skinned angels, are reluctant to open their mouths to this modern slavery.

From softcore porn, people are slowly turning to hardcore porn. There is a growing demand for more extremes, more oppression of women, more perverted sex. At the same time live webcam sex, live rape is increasing. Compared to "independent" women, trafficked sex workers are less troublesome and less costly. In a word, the most important thing for human traffickers to make money through the sense industry is to teach men that women are just commodities. You have the right to eat as much as you want. And is there any better way to instill this belief in a man's brain than through pornography?

Once a young man came to the Prophet (5) and said, "O Messenger of Allah, allow me to commit adultery." Everyone present was shocked to hear this, but Rasulullah called him with affection. He asked her, "Would you like it for your mother?"

The young man said, "No, O Messenger of Allah. May Allah dedicate me to you. No one would like that for his mother. "

Rasulullah (d) asked the young man one by one, then for your daughter?

For your sister? For your fukura? For your aunt? The young man said every time, no man would like it.

Then the Prophet (*) laid his hands on his body and prayed: "O Allah, forgive him his sins, purify his heart and protect his character. "After receiving this lesson from the Prophet (i), the young man did not look up when he was walking on the road in his later life."

My brother, believe me, behind the fantasy of every porn video is the helpless screams of many men and women, the sighs rising from the depths of my chest, the story of breaking many unknown dreams. Because you and countless others like you watch porn videos, because you create demand by downloading porn from the net, these helpless women, children have to fall prey to human traffickers, have to choose a horrible life. Maybe your mouse click on a porn website is ruining one's world. Any of you Close relatives, can you guarantee that your sister will never be the victim of such horrors any day?

What is the need for momentary pleasure, temporary excitement to poison the free air of this world?

Embers

One.

Tall, upright body structure.

Curly hair, erect nose like eagle's lips.

Handsome. Dashing.

8 students of law Humble, humble, elegant taste-dress, all in all a very attractive personality. A decent gentleman from head to toe. At first glance, anyone is forced to choose. Eyes full of mystery and Maya's strangeness are enough to deprive any girl of a good night's sleep.

There was another animal hiding behind the handsome face and the gentleman's mask. It's as if he's a real doctor, Jekyll and Mr. Hyde, from Robert Louis Stevenson's storybook. He was a serial killer, rapist, vampire. It is known for sure that he killed more than 30 girls with his own hands. Although the actual number is supposed to be much higher. Serial killers have all kinds of whims. Her whim was necrophilia sex with corpses. He used to rape the corpses of his victims until they started rotting.

Name given by parents, Theodore Robert Bundy. People knew him as Ted Bundy. He was cunning like a fox, his movements were as silent as a cat. The woman had a perfect hunting plan. Cheetahs would hunt in the air like ghosts. Bagha Bagha police officers and veteran detectives left tears and tears in their eyes. In the seventies, a state of terror was established in 6 states of America.

First Hit

Exactly when and where Bundy started hunting has been extensively investigated, much water has been muddied, but the actual information has not been able to come out. Bundy used to talk to different people from time to time.

Although kidnapping and rape of girls is thought to have started in 1989, Bundy's murder and necrophilia began in 1981. Due to some clues, and some information found in the investigation, many detectives think that Bandi's handcuffs as a murderer are much earlier. By killing an 8-year-old girl in 1971. Bandi was only 14 then. Bundy, however, has always denied the allegations.

After a few kidnappings and a couple of murders, Bundy started his real game. In 1974, at the age of 26.

The victim

Bundy used to target beautiful girls studying in college and university in attractive clothes of the latest fashion. Whose age is usually between 15-25 years. After getting dressed in fashionable clothes, masks, torch lights, ropes, straight sticks, handcuffs, etc., were loaded on brown Volkswagen and Bundy would go out in search of prey. I used to patrol in places where women are more frequent. If he remembered someone or saw a beautiful woman walking on the road alone, he would get out of the car.

One hand was hanging on the sling or one leg was plastered — pretending to break his arm / leg. In the other hand there was a heavy briefcase or a thick book. To get too close to the target, he would drop the books aloud to attract attention or think that the briefcase was too hard to carry urgent help was needed. In order to help the target, the handsome bundy used to "just soak and soak". Requested to bring briefcases or books to the car. As soon as he reached the car, hell would come down on the head of the target. After a few days, the body of the helpless girl could be found in a secluded, abandoned place — in the mountains or in the forest without her disfigured clothes. Many times no trace of the body could be found. Bundy used to have sex with corpses until the corpses began to rot. Maybe he would kill in one place and come to an area 200 miles away and kill another. Then he came to the first crime spot and rubbed salt on the corpse - the devil in the form of a pure human.

The girls in Seattle, Salt Lake City, Colorado, Florida were terrified. An unknown psycho is roaming the city, I don't know whose turn it is. The girls would disappear on the way from one hostel to another, on the way back from the theater or cinema hall, even from one room to another through the corridor, the killer could not be caught by combing operations. One girl after another is mysteriously disappearing but there is no end to the mystery, the killer is not being caught. Detectives from the King County Sheriff's Office and the Seattle Police Department went crazy to catch the culprit. But no one realized until the number of Bundy's victims was over twenty, they were all actually running after one man individually.

The reason was, of course. Ted Bundy's brain was sharp, he could analyze the situation and make decisions very quickly. An in-depth study of crime methodology taught him how to become a hopscotch instantly without leaving a fingerprint or any such clue at the crime spot without raising any suspicion.

The master was in disguise he could change his appearance very quickly by running two fingers through his hair or changing facial expressions. No eyewitness could accurately describe his appearance to the police. He did not use a gun on purpose to hide his identity. Instead, he used household chores — nylon ropes, stockings ...

He carried out murders and rapes in such a small area in such a short period of time that it was not possible for the police to understand that only one person was responsible for all these hellish incidents. In Bundy's own words,

"(I am) the most cold-hearted son of ab *** h you'll ever meet ... No one can say exactly how many murders Bundy committed in total. Evidence suggests that the number of victims in Bundy may be close to one hundred.Bundy's personal lawyer testified that Bundy himself confessed to him that he had committed more than a hundred murders.

Shrighar Darshan

The girls of several states are mysteriously lost one after another. It is not possible to rescue anyone alive. A few days later, the mutilated body was found. The FBI has set a trap to catch the killer, but the killer is cleverly breaking through the net each time.

August, 1985. The Utah Highway is a short distance from Salt Lake City, USA. A brown Volkswagen was stopped for missing a traffic signal. There is next to the driver's seat in front of the astonished officers saw bhauksaoyyaganera. The suspect was searched inside the car. Nylon ropes, sledgehammers, handcuffs, masks, gloves, screwdrivers and other trinkets were found. "This guy can't be a burglar," thought the patrol officers.

Ekan-Okan tried to convince the officers with a wide-eyed smile - the Bersik officers handcuffed him and he exchanged laughter. Officers did not yet know that the man they had just arrested was one of America's top ten most wanted people. Theodore Robert Bundy aka Ted Bundy, killing women by strangling them like animals, then eating the corpse like a vampire whose addiction.

Where is Gone?

Bundy was taken from Garfield County Jail to Pitkin County Courthouse for a hearing in June 1966. Bundy was given a chance to defend himself. The handcuffs were opened. At one point during the break, Bundy went to the library to study his case. Go to the library for a book from the shelf behind the jump out of a window on the ground storey. The ankle sprained but was able to move beyond the boundaries of the court

Aspen tries to escape through the mountains to avoid the roadblock given by the police. But lost its way in the hilly areas. Six days later, exhausted, Bundy surrendered to the police. After returning to the jail, Bundy started plotting to escape again. Raised one for about 500 dollar Hack's Blade. In the evening, the other prisoners started leaking the ceiling of their cells while taking a bath. After six months of relentless effort and a weight loss of 16 kg, Bundy was able to climb the ceiling through a hole of about one foot square. With several rehearsals, he prepared himself to escape from prison.

The night of December 30, 1986. Most of the prison staff are on Christmas break. Bundy took advantage of this opportunity. Out of the hole in the ceiling, the air is instantly released from the jail. 16 hours later, on December 31, when prison officials discovered the hole in the ceiling of Bundy's cell, Bundy Pogarpar.

On The Brink of Death

Bundy escaped from prison and arrived in Florida. The FBI and Florida police continue to use the thumbs up to commit a series of rapes and heinous murders.

Finally Ted near Alabama State on February 12 at 1 p.m.

Bundy was arrested by police officer David Lee. Mr. With Lee Bundy straight

Go to jail. On the way, Bundy said to himself, "You killed me

To do well, officer. "

Ted Bundy was sentenced to death for his crime.

Ted Bundy was executed on January 24, 1989 at 8:17 a.m. local time in an electric chair. At that time about two thousand people had gathered outside the jail. Most were young women and girls.

They were dancing, singing, setting off fireworks, chanting slogans like "Burn Bundy Burn", "Ted, you're dead!" Bundy's body was cremated and cremated at an undisclosed location in Washington.

What was the driving force of this dark world of Bandi? Why couldn't a higher university degree make Ted Bundy human?

How did a man become so perverted? Will have to wait a little longer to find out ...

Two

Uttar Pradesh.

India.

A schoolgirl is sitting in a secluded field.

He is surrounded by a lustful man. The girl is trembling in an impossible way, looking around again and again with wide eyes like a trapped deer. Feeling we have 'Run out of gas' emotionally. But no, the last was not saved. One laughed like a wild boar. A human-like animal jumped on him.

It is hard to believe that someone would upload a video of this heinous crime of torturing a helpless girl in turn and upload it online and thousands or millions of people would see it and satisfy their eyes and hands. Is it possible for people to go down so low?

Are all the poems written in praise of humanity for ages false?

But such incidents are happening all over the world, especially in Uttar Pradesh, India. According to the Times of India, videos of rape of helpless girls at the tip of the nose by the police and the administration are being sold in shops in Uttar Pradesh, India. Hundreds, if not thousands, of rape videos are being sold every day at prices ranging from Rs 50 to Rs 150.

Fifty to one and a half hundred, that's the price of a girl's honor! "You know, I probably know the girl in this new hot video," says a man to a boy in a store who has just begun to grow a mustache. The video shows a girl in her late twenties torturing two animals. The helpless girl's voice is full of longing, "I'm sorry, I'm sorry." At least the video is crazy. "

According to a senior police officer, the rape scene was videotaped

To blackmail the victim. This is confirmed by various sources in the police It has happened that the administration will not be able to stop these heinous incidents.

The culture of rape has become epidemic in India. One rape is being committed every 20 minutes. India is in the top ten of the list of countries with the highest number of rapes in the world. In addition, there were many cases of child prostitution and child sexual abuse in India. There have been many reports in the media in many countries of the world.

There are even five cases of child sexual abuse in the world

India's name is also in the shortlist of the country.

Three

August, 2013. USA. Land of dreams, freedom and liberty. Sara (pseudonym) who has just turned 19 is very happy today. His dream is going to be fulfilled. After many attempts, I finally got the opportunity to study at the university of my choice. The long awaited moment has come. On the second night of campus, all the classmates were partying together. Sara was there too. The hands of the clock have touched twelve houses long ago.

One male classmate was met. Although I have never seen the boy before, there have been occasional online conversations. After chatting for a while, the boy suggested, "Come on, let's have some drinks." Sara shook her head and said, "You're right, your throat is dry and has become wood." The boy poured the drink into a glass. Sara sipped on the glass. Then I don't remember anything ...

Nine hours later, when she regained consciousness, she found herself in an unfamiliar bed. The head was tingling, not even a thread on the body. The hair is messy. There is a boy sitting in a chair next to the bed. This boy poured wine into her glass last night, Sarah remembered. A medical checkup report from a local hospital confirmed that Sara had been raped. 185

Such incidents are very common in European-American educational institutions. Rape is very common among students in Europe and America. It is true that world-renowned educational institutions are creating many people who have changed the history of the world, but at the same time they are creating many rapists and more. Western school, college, university campuses are the most unsafe campuses in the world for women. The words may seem exaggerated but hopefully some statistics will help to understand the horrors of the situation:

A 2007 survey found that American college and university students had been raped at least once in their lives. 1 involved in rape. One in three female students in England is raped in her own school. Half of the undergraduate female students said they all knew someone who had been raped by their friends on campus.

In January 2014, the then President of the United States Barack Obama

Admittedly, statistics show that 1 out of every 5 female students on American college campuses has been raped. 160 A new one published in 2015 by the Association of American Universities. The report shows that one in four people before graduation

John was raped by a woman. The report has been made 26 top

The survey was conducted among about one and a half lakh students of the university.

The report paints a grim picture of violence against women in American educational institutions from a previous report in 2014 (the Obama administration's White House Task Force to Protect Students from Sexual Assault) to ensure the safety of female students on campus.

However, the White House task force's first report, 71, said three out of four female students were sexually abused while on campus.

Sarah has not made any formal complaint to the police against her rapist.

Who raped her was never made public. It is not uncommon in America for such incidents to be suppressed. According to the American Civil Liberties Union, no complaints were filed after 95 percent of the rapes on campus.

And even if rape is alleged, due to legal and administrative complications, in most cases, the rapist does not even get a flower.

Four

"Female members of the US Army are more concerned about being sexually harassed by their male colleagues than they are about enemies ..."

Dora Hernandez, who is almost ten years old, said the words with a deep sigh. For a long time that work has been in the American Navy and Army National Guard.Dora Hernandez and several other women returning to Iraq and Afghanistan talking to. This is against the most formidable and reckless fighters in the world though somehow able to defend themselves on the fronts, throughout the entire career they have had to fight another war in silence — and in that war they have fought again and again.

Has been defeated. Their silent war against rape. The Pentagon's own research shows that there are four people in the US military one of the female members was sexually abused throughout her career.

Sabina Radangel opened her mouth after Dora Hernandez stopped. "I was sexually abused when I was in an army boot camp," she said in the drawing room of Sabina's home near El Paso, Texas. "Then when I went to the Navy, I was raped."

Jamie Livingstone, who has served in the US Navy for more than six years, said: "I knew the culture of the US Army was that soldiers and officers had a right to rape. So I would suppress the incidents of rape. And my boss used to rape me, so who should I complain to? "

One by one, these women were reporting incidents of sexual abuse with them in the American Army. None of them are acquaintances, but the painful experience of being sexually harassed by their colleagues and bosses in the American Army has brought them closer to each other. They were sharing each other's sorrows by opening all the windows of their hearts. 1984 according to Pentagon figures, only 14 percent of all sexual assaults within the US military involved in world peace are reported. The remaining 6 percent of the incidents remain hidden from public view. According to the Pentagon's 2010 census, there are 19,000 in the U.S. Army each year. Incidents of sexual abuse occur. In 2011 the number increased to twenty six thousand. In 2017, the number is 60,000! Female members of the U.S. military are at greater risk of sexual abuse than American civilian women.

Even male members of the U.S. Army are sexually abused and raped by colleagues. In some cases, the amount is higher than women. But in very few cases these incidents are reported. "We must change this culture of rape," said Gary Patton, head of the Pentagon's Office of Sexual Assault Prevention and Response. Sexual abuse should not be accepted as normal. Everyone in the victim's unit must take the issue of sexual abuse very seriously.

Not only that, but the children of their colleagues and subordinates are not safe in the hands of the members of the US Army engaged in the rescue of the world and the establishment of human rights. 189 In 2014, the United States Army officially reported the abuse of six children (the children of their colleagues). 190 It is assumed that the number of unreported cases is even higher.

Five

The cruelty in the name of rape is increasing alarmingly day by day in Bangladesh. Not only women but also children and teenagers are being victimized by this barbarism. Not only rape or gang rape, murder is also being brutally committed. For the last few months, there has been a celebration of rape and murder after rape. The statistics of the concerned agencies are also giving identical information. According to multiple agencies, the average number of rapes per year in the last six years is More than that happened in 6 months of 2017. As such, this heinous crime is now doubling.

On November 30, 2016, a heretic named Shipon murdered Tanha, a 3-year-old and 9-month-old child, after raping her in the capital's Badda. On July 17 of the same year, Tufan Sarkar raped a female student in Bogra in the name of college admission. When justice is sought, the heads of mothers and daughters are disgustingly shaved. There were multiple rapes and murders in late November and early December. A university student has been gang-raped in Rajshahi. In Narayanganj, a teenager was raped by a driver and a helper in a moving truck. A ninth-grade relative strangled 7-year-old Farzana to death after she was raped in Keraniganj in September.

Thus, every day women are being raped somewhere in the country. The "girl child" under the age of 18 is not exempt. Surprisingly, even three- or four-year-old infants are victims of this perverted sex. Rape is also being killed after rape. But the victim is not disclosing the lion's share of these incidents for fear of public embarrassment. Their families are hiding it for fear of social stigma. The case is not going on for fear of procrastination and harassment of influential people. Rather, the victim and their family are being pressured in such a way that nothing has happened for fear of being known. Even then, the number of incidents that are being revealed is scary. According to various government and non-government organizations, the number of rapes has doubled this year as compared to the last six years. This image is the same in the capital city Dhaka as in the whole country. The brutality of some of these rapes is shocking everyone.

Farida Yasmin, deputy commissioner (DC) of the Dhaka Metropolitan Police's Women Support and Investigation Division, said she was tasked with investigating sensitive cases involving rape of women and children. More such cases are coming now than in the past. Rape of women and children has also increased.

According to the Bangladesh Human Rights Implementation Agency (BMBS), the rate of rape has been steadily rising since 2012 (excluding 2014). In 2012, 60 women were raped, 30 were murdered after being raped and 26 women were gang-raped. In 2013, 106 women were raped, 17 women were murdered after being raped and 35 women were gang-raped. In 2014, 153 women were raped, 46 were murdered and 6 were gang-raped. In 2015, 134 rapes, 46 rapes were followed by murders and 103 women were gang-raped. In 2016, 141 women were raped and 33 were raped Murder and 6 people have been gang raped. In the first six months till June this year, 141 women have been raped and 43 gang-raped. After the rape, 14 victims had to give their lives.

The number of child rapes, gang rapes and murders has not been less in recent years. 115 children were raped in 2014, 141 in 2015 and 156 in 2016. In the first six months of 2016, 144 children were raped. Last year, a total of 299 women and children were raped (alone), but this year the number has risen to 265 in six months. Not only that. The company's latest report suggests a sense of dread. According to the report, 60 women and children were raped in July 2016. Of which 32 are children. And 3 children have been killed after being raped. 199

Why is the great festival of rape going on around the world today? Why are women constantly being persecuted in our "great civilization" of women's liberties and individual liberties? Why is the security of women so endangered in the Western world, which has given the world all the rights of women and women's freedom?

Why are women being raped at incredible rates in Western universities, factories that build "free-minded" "free people" and maternity wards of free thought? Why is an American being sexually abused every 96 seconds?

Why is 1 in 8 women in America and 1 in 33 men being raped at least once in their lives?

Why are members of the American Army and their children not safe from the sexual violence of the American Army, which is waging a global "war on terror" against Muslims? Why are so many rapes happening in a conservative country like Bangladesh?

Why is the procession of corpses of raped women increasing as the country moves forward in tandem with the world? Why?

Six

An experiment on rape-propensity was conducted at the University of Manitoba. One group of men is shown rape porn and the other group is shown non-rape porn. They are then asked to arouse themselves to the maximum level without any hand touch. It turned out that the fantasies of those who were shown rape porn were more barbaric and full of sexual violence than the rest.

But the relationship to violence is not just about rape porn. Studies have shown that there is a direct link between pornography and any form of porn of abuse, drugs, alcohol, and sexual aggression. All this is enough to rape someone at the right time and situation. So those who watch hardcore porn, there is a huge possibility that they will turn into rape

The issue of the relationship between pornography and rape and sexual violence has come up in many experiments. An analysis of data from 100 women who were sexually abused by the Rape Crisis Center found that 28 percent said they were watching abusive porn. Twelve percent said the rapist was trying to mimic a porn video scene during their rape.

Even domestic violence is influenced by pornography. Gold Coast Center Against Sexual 109/234 The level of abuse at the hands of family members has risen sharply in Australia. Pornography is one of the factors behind this. Rape of women, forced group sex, suffocation during sex, beatings - nothing is left out. Their husbands or boyfriends who are addicted to porn have carried out all these acts of violence and aggression. The level of torture is so horrific that in most cases women have to be admitted to hospital emergencies.

Studies have shown that the free spread of pornography has a direct effect on the increase in sexual violence and rape.

The South Australian administration once adopted a more liberal approach to pornography. Although making, promoting and selling porn videos is prohibited by law, it is the administration

Time adopts the principle of being blindfolded. He pretended not to see. The result?

Rape in South Australia increased by 264%.

At the same time, the administration in Queensland, Australia, has taken a hard line against pornography. A few days later, the Queensland administration saw a 23% increase in rape cases. Hawaii also once adopted a liberal approach to pornography. A few days later, the administration took very strict action against pornography. Then again liberalism. Analyzing the results, it was found that the level of rape was much higher when liberalism was adopted in the field of pornography. The level of rape decreased when the administration resorted to austerity. The next time the level of rape increased after the re-adoption of liberalism. That is, the proportion of sexual violence and rape is proportional to the number and availability of pornography. When the availability of pornography is high, the rate of sexual violence and rape also increases. When the availability of pornography decreases, the rate of sexual violence and rape decreases.

Many may object that not everyone who views pornography is involved in rape or sexual violence. That's true. But there is a "but". While not everyone who views pornography is involved in rape or sexual violence, more than 99% of those who view rape view pornography. Besides, whether pornography makes a rapist or not is not our main point. Rather, the conclusion that has been repeatedly drawn from these studies is that pornography tends to lead to rape, sexual violence, and perverted sex among viewers. Just as the proliferation of hardcore pornography increases the prevalence of anal sex and oral sex at an alarming rate, so does the prevalence of rape and sexual violence. It may be easier to understand if you think of rape as a perverted sex rather than as a crime for a while. Another notable issue is that incidents of rape and sexual violence involve questions of appropriate context, time and opportunity. In most cases, such crimes are opportunistic. This is why rapists and sexual oppressors are called Sexual Predators. Such criminals are like opportunistic predators. What pornography does is create a tendency to rape in viewers and create an acceptance of rape in their minds. Many of them may not realize the fantasy of rape due to lack of proper opportunity and context, but it cannot be said that they will not do it if proper context is created.

Think of it this way. What would happen if thousands of porn-addicted young people were isolated from society, separated from their wives or girlfriends, and given a conducive environment for rape where there was no fear of accountability or punishment?

The answer lies in the American military's culture of rape and child labor. Pornography in military camps has been cited as a reason for the ongoing rape and sexual abuse in the US military, especially the availability of softcore porn magazines and online pornography. The sale of these magazines in military camps has been banned to reduce the rate of sexual abuse.

The Joint Chiefs of Staff said, "This is what we have in our forces the culture of sexual abuse must change. And that's why the military the sale of pornographic magazines has been banned in the bases.However many are skeptical about how much the move will improve the situation. Because, Porn sites can be easily accessed from the camps. Seen in 200 studies one out of every ten American civilians is on the Internet addicted to pornography. But the rate of porn-addiction among members of the military much more. According to American Navy Lieutenant Michael Howard at least 20% of members of the military are addicted to Internet porn according to the priests of the military, those to whom the members of the army regularly belong Internet porn addiction is at the top of the list of personal problems faced by members of the U.S. military who confess to personal sins. Pornographic videos and pictures of children are regularly found on the computers of members of the U.S. military. For this reason, army members and officers have also been punished at different times. Six U.S. Air Force paratroopers have been punished in 2008 for participating in 202 gay porn videos and publishing them on gay porn websites. Of course the history of homosexuality and homosexual pornography in the American military is quite old.

India is another example of the interrelationship between pornography and rape. India ranks third in the list of countries with the highest number of Internet pornography viewers. India also ranks third in the world in terms of the number of female viewers of porn. On the other hand, India ranks fifth in the list of countries with the highest number of rape cases.

However, a specialty of India is the popularity of rape porn here.

A 2014 survey found that 40 percent of men in the Indian state of Goa watch "rape porn." 7% of them admitted that rape porn made them want to rape. 48% said that once they saw rape porn, they started watching child pornography. The survey was conducted in the case of undergraduate students of ten universities. So there is no lack of "higher education" or any excuse to make such an excuse. It is affecting the society and the behavior of the people in the society. And thus these factors are playing a role behind the increasing rape in India. It cannot be said that the situation in Bangladesh is very good in comparison.

Rape is on the rise in Bangladesh at an alarming rate. And one of the most influential behind this is pornography. That's what experts say. Chairman of the Department of Psychotherapy at the National Institute of Mental Health. Mohit Kamal told the daily Manabjamin that the number of rapes is increasing in our recent observations as well as the statistics of the agencies. Pictures and videos of sex between men and women, and pornographic pornography starring pornographers are reaching out hand in hand. Seeing that, adults and minors are not able to control their sexual instincts. Recklessly becoming consumerist. As a result, instead of conquering women through love, marriage, etc. and establishing normal sexual relations, they are raping unprotected women and children. Among the many reasons, it is now the main reason for the increase in rape of women and children, he said.

Sigma Huda, chairman of the Bangladesh Human Rights Implementation Organization (BMBS), said the country was in a state of social and political instability. At the same time pornography has spread hand in hand. For these reasons, women and children are being raped, gang-raped and murdered from time to time.

Numerous such studies have proven the role of pornography and the sexuality of society in the effects of pornography behind the increase in rape by 210. Porn-addiction has definitely been proven to be one of the causes of rape. "I'm just watching, I'm not doing anything", "There is no harm in watching porn" - so I hope you will remember these studies once before saying such things.

In addition, the study conducted on 18-19 year old adolescents yes, porn addiction incites children and adolescents to sexual violence 42% of teenagers accustomed to watching porn are sexually harassed in one way or another.

The rate of hardcore porn addiction is very high among sex offenders. 8% of child sex offenders or pedophiles, 53% of forced incest victims and 69% of rapists are addicted to hardcore pornography.

Pornography is very popular among serial killers and rapists.

John Douglas, a former FBI officer, wrote in his book Journey Into Darkness that pornographic videos are usually found in the dens of serial killers and rapists. Charles Lindecker's Thrill Killers, a Study of America's Most Vicious Murders, reports that 61% of such killers say that pornography is the primary object of their sexual desire.

Members of the law enforcement agencies, which have been directly involved in cracking down on sex offenders and rapists, have unanimously acknowledged the link between rape and sexual harassment and pornography. There are reasons. They have found evidence of the depth of the relationship between such crimes and criminals.

Retired Detective of the New York Police Department and New York founder of the Detective Bureau's Criminal Assessment and

Profiling Unit here are excerpts from an interview with Raymond Pierce:

Q: In light of your experience, do you believe that sex offenders are more likely to watch porn than ordinary people?

Raymond Pierce: My experience is that such criminals have a habit of watching porn at a deadly rate. I can't talk about the habit of watching porn with ordinary people, but different types of pornography are within their reach.

There have been many times when the culprit of a serious crime whether the crime is sexual or whatever has been caught and when asked, "Well, where have you been in the last four days? What have you done? " They are replying, "I have committed a crime, I have to escape." When asked, "Where did you go?" The answer is, "I took a room in a cheap motel, then rented a prostitute" or "I took a room in a motel that shows porn 24 hours a day ...". This is how they relax. Tension is relieved.

Question: Can you give us an idea of the percentage of sex in your investigation?

Got pornography from criminals?

Pierce: It's not possible to say thorns, but you don't have to ask a lot of times, it just comes out. My colleagues and I used to say, "Here's another one ... they seem to be doing just that ..." I would say we have found pornography in more than 75% of criminals. The number can be 100%.

Question: You mentioned our research on imprisoned pedophiles (child pornography, child sexual abuse) and their sexuality. What do you say about their porn addiction? And what about the use of porn before committing such a crime?

Pierce: Suppose a male pedophile, that attacks little boys by In their case I use the word "attack", although they think so that they are not attacking the children. According to their distorted mentality.They assume that they are targeting children through these attacks I have seen the effects of pornography on their sexual crimes are quite instructive, what I know about them, maybe they had a job, eight hours or ten hours a day. But in every waking moment, these fantasies were going on in their heads. As long as she is awake, working, she is constantly imagining child rape, sexual abuse. And the porn videos they have, they serve as the fuel for these fantasies.

Seven

I started with Bundy. Let's do the last one with him ...

Pornography was one of the driving forces behind the dark world of the terrifying monster serial killer Ted Bundy. Twelve-thirteen-year-old Ted Bundy found pornographic magazines in grocery stores and drug stores outside his home, the same day little Ted was born a rapist.

Ted Bundy gave an interview to psychologist James C. Dobson on January 24, 1969, shortly before his death. In this interview she discusses in detail how pornography turned her into an animal.

Not to mention Ted Bundy's remarks on the brink of death: "... None of us who are heavily influenced by media violence, especially pornographic violence, are outwardly monsters. We are your sons, your husbands. And like everyone else, we grew up in a family structure. But now it has become such a thing that pornography enters anyone's home and in one fell swoop takes the child out of the family structure. Just like twenty or thirty years ago it kicked me out. My parents were sincere in protecting their children from this, as is the case with other hardline Christian families, but society is very relaxed about these external influences. "

... I am not a sociologist and I will not pretend that I believe in the traditional ideas of civilized society. But I have been in prison for a long time and during this time I have met many people who are motivated to commit violence. With few exceptions, each of them was deeply addicted to pornography. The FBI's own homicide report says pornography is of general interest to serial killers. So there is no way to ignore it.

I hope that those who have caused irreparable harm to me will not believe in my remorse but will believe the words I will say now. Our city, our community is very relaxed about some of the influencers who have far-reaching harmful effects. Today or tomorrow these will be published. Violence in the media, especially sexual violence, is now being swallowed up in various ways. I get scared when I watch cable TV. Nowadays the violence that reaches our drawing room through movies Thirty years ago, they were not even shown in X-rated adult theaters.

"... As I have said before, the laxity of our society towards (these) influencers is obvious. Especially this kind of violent pornography. When civilized society walks around blaming Ted Bundy on porn magazines pretending not to see them, a group of young people are actually turning to Ted Bundy without their knowledge. The place of regret is right here. "216

The three notable characteristics of psychopathic serial killers are: being able to lie very convincingly, not feeling any remorse and not admitting one's guilt under any circumstances, blaming someone or something else in one way or another. Bundy's last words can be dismissed as the remorseless excuse of a cold-headed serial killer. But in light of the reality we see around the world almost three decades after this January 1979 interview - a very small fraction of which we have come up with in this article Bundy was right.

As much as the shackles of lies

By this time, I hope you understand the relationship between pornography and sex crimes. Pornography directly acts as an influencer of perverted sex and sexual harassment. Sexuality is as physical as it is emotional. Pornography targets the human mind, and once it affects the mind, it begins to make an impression on the body. Everyone who is addicted to pornography comes out and starts raping, that's not the case. However, by changing the normal perception of porn sex, it creates the desire for perverted and abnormal sex. The acceptance of perverted sex is created in everyone who is addicted to pornography.

A lot of things will seem unusual, dirty to you when watching hardcore pornography for the first time. The body will tingle. But if you are constantly watching such porn videos, at some point you will find these things very normal. Not only that, you will be attracted to such behavior. Pornography thus creates a variety of obsessive and pathological tendencies in us.

Different types of addiction, obsession, disorder or pathological behavior are formed in each person. It could be masturbation, virulence, perverted sex like 218 anal-oral sex, suffering from constant sexual fantasies, group sex, homosexuality, childishness, rape tendency, widespread polygamy or any other sexual-mental perversion.

Simply put, pornography destroys people's normal sexual orientation. The more "strict" the style of pornography, the more intense its impact on viewers. Due to the widespread presence of violence in today's most popular porn videos, rape is on the rise among porn addicts. No one with common sense should disagree with these words. A person whose fitrah (natural disposition) has not been ruined, will accept these words. But the problem is elsewhere.

In economics. When the economy falls into an equation, even the most straightforward issues become extremely confusing. The hundreds of billions of dollars in questions associated with the global pornography industry. 2006

The total revenue of the industry in the year was 96 billion dollars. More than the combined revenue of Microsoft, Google, Amazon, Yahoo, Apple and Netflix! In 218 years, the profit of the porn industry is 15 billion dollars. He's Hollywood's annual in comparison

Profit? 10 billion. |

And this is just the calculation of declared income. A large part of the transactions in the porn industry are never reported. 220 means the actual size of the industry is even bigger. When so much money is involved with something, it becomes very difficult to admit it as harmful, to declare it. The simple equation gets into a messy economy. Protecting the golden-eyed swan has become a question of bread and capital. The industries of pharmaceuticals, hotels and tours, cable and satellite television networks, Wall Street, global sex trafficking, sexology and psychology all benefit in various ways through the porn industry.

In order to hide the harmful effects of porn on individuals and society, mass propaganda is used to prove that porn is innocent and useful entertainment. And many who are caught in the trap of pornography and masturbation are constantly blinded by these gaps.

One such widely used theory is the "Catharsis Theory" or "Catharsis Effect". Referring to this theory over and over again, many claim, "Pornography does not only act as an influencer of rape, sexual abuse, sexual perversion, mental disorder, child pornography, but it is very effective in reducing the level of these crimes in society. Absolutely Brahmastra! "

So how does this Brahmastra work?

Proponents of this theory explain it this way—

Suppose someone is very restless in the heat of work. Insane state. There is a risk of disaster if you can't be intimate with anyone in any way. But that person has no chance to be intimate with anyone. What will he do now? Exhausted by the constant torture of instinct, he can raise his hand to any woman around him, it is not impossible to look at the children, he can even go to the brothel! But if he has the opportunity to watch porn, then he can cool down by releasing the ever-increasing pressure inside him. Countless people of the society will be saved from disaster.

Suppose a person is a potential child rapist. For a long time his desire was to oppress children. But it is not possible due to lack of opportunity. Now if this person is constantly shown child porn, he will lose interest in having sex with children after a while.In this way, people's sexual harassment, sexual perversion, desire for sexual harassment, sex fantasies will be fulfilled by watching porn. In real life you will no longer need to do these perverted things. Society will be saved from loss.

After reading so far, I think it's right! Pornography saves society from catastrophe by creating a safe way to satisfy sexual needs (no matter how perverted).

But in fact the opposite is true. This theory was rejected by the experts long ago

Dropped in the book. So where is the gap of Subhankar?

The experimental setup of the experiment on which Catharsis Theory was based was very messy. Nothing has been done about the standards that need to be maintained for quality and acceptable research. A 15-day study of just over 30 people (32 people) in Tenetun Continuation draws the conclusion of Catharsis Theory. Out of these 32 people, a group of 23 people were shown porn videos of the same genre for 15 days and 90 minutes continuously. After 15 days, the group of 23 people said that at first they were excited to watch porn videos, but later they lost interest in porn videos. As a result of watching similar porn videos, they get bored. Shubhankar's hoax is here. Rather than justifying porn, it is actually evidence of the horrific harmful effects of porn on human sexuality.

Think about it. 15 days of similar porn; After only 15 days, people start to feel bored. The same style of porn can no longer arouse them as before. Suppose you like to eat biryani, now if you have to be fed biryani continuously for a few days, then at some point you will not want to eat biryani anymore. That's normal. Similarly, it is very normal to lose interest in porn videos of the same genre if you watch them again and again.

What can people do to get rid of monotony in such a situation? Do they become bored and stop watching porn? Or does pornography have no effect on their behavior and sexual needs? But we already understand that sexual desire is affected to some extent. Because, after watching porn for a few days, the viewer's ability to get aroused is decreasing, sensitivity is decreasing.

People usually watch softcore porn at first. At one point, softcore porn began to bore them. Then they turn to hardcore pornography. Even hardcore pornography at one time is not enough to arouse them. The porn-addict then tends toward more rigorous pornography. Extremely perverted types of pornography such as animal sex, child pornography, rape porn, taboo, etc. began to be seen. This means that while watching porn, it keeps increasing. At the beginning of the addiction, if someone watches one hour of porn a week, after a while he will probably watch two hours of porn a week, thus gradually increasing the amount of porn viewing. At the same time, there is a strong desire to imitate the things seen on the screen in real life.

Now one might say, "Do all those who watch porn start rape or child abuse? Of course not. So it is wrong to say that pornography affects rape or other sexual perversions. "

This is like the false claim of the tobacco industry that "since many smokers do not die of lung cancer, smoking is not the cause of lung cancer." It is true that not everyone goes out to rape after watching porn videos. But does this lead to the conclusion that porn actually prevents rape? Let's look at two important questions.

1. What do people usually do after watching pornography?

2. Is viewing pornography any psychosexual Affect?

Everyone knows the answer to the first question. No one goes back to studying, doing office work or talking to family members after watching porn. You must be "cold" after watching porn. If for some reason it is not possible then, in a little seclusion, the person wants to be "cold" as soon as he gets the right opportunity. Most people masturbate after watching porn and in most cases porn is viewed to masturbate. It's like a circular loop.

Although for most people masturbation may be a "lower quality" alternative to sex than sex, masturbation at the end of the day is still a sexual act. So we all agree that people watch porn to have sex (masturbate) or watch porn to arouse themselves before sex. Watching porn, listening to music or watching dramas is not just passive, passive entertainment. Rather, watching porn is part of a process with which real sex is inextricably linked. After watching porn, you will find the release. That's normal. Pornography and the pleasure of ejaculation, tied together. Ejaculation or reaching orgasm through sexual intercourse is a natural consequence of watching porn.

If you admit this, then the question is, do you think that in all cases this "sexual activity" will be limited to masturbation? Porn-addicted people will only be interested in masturbation? Keep thinking, in that gap we take a look at the answer to the second question.

Does viewing pornography have a psychosexual effect on the viewer?

Yes. Pornography affects the sexual psychology of the viewer. This can be proved by the theory that is used to prove that pornography is beneficial. Boredom of watching the same type of porn over and over again is a sexual-psychological change. What the audience used to be excited about is no longer what it used to be, it is the result of a sexual-psychological change. Due to porn, the sexual desires and sexual thoughts of the viewers are changing.

Ordinary sexual behavior, apart from the sex scenes seen in porn, seems to be absolutely pansy to many porn-addicts. For many, it becomes difficult to get aroused naturally without porn or perverted sex, this is another proof. This is further proof that porn addicts want to imitate what they see in real life porn videos.

People are not only getting released by watching porn, they are also developing a strong desire for special types of sex and only then the catharsis theory is proved wrong. 228

One point here is that the effects of pornography on sexual psychology are not immediately effective. Those who say that pornography is beneficial, they want to prove their claim based on this point. But the problem is that they avoid the long-term effects of pornography. No one goes out to rape after watching porn, but that doesn't mean it doesn't have any effect on him. The effects of pornography on sexual psychology are slowly gaining ground. Day after day, month after month, as a result of watching pornography again and again, the structure of his thinking changes.

A porn-addict cannot be aroused without watching porn or fantasizing about porn scenes. Again, if he continues to watch porn, his ability to get aroused through porn also decreases with time. She can't be aroused without more violent, more perverted porn. If this process continues, at some point his thoughts about sex will suddenly become detached from the normal sexual behavior of real life. In simple terms, pornography is the first thing that motivates people to have sex. And secondly, pornography changes people's preference for sex. Her sexuality and sexual psychology become distorted. On the one hand, intense sexual desire works in him, on the other hand, it becomes almost impossible for him to be naturally satisfied. His attitudes and behavior towards women, marriage, sex, rape, perverted sex, etc. change. Such a person is more likely to be involved in rape, child sex or any other perverted sex.

"Starting with cigarettes, heroin in the end", that's a lot. This is the classic pattern of drug addiction. In the beginning it becomes a little intoxicating. But over time, that is likely to increase. More drugs are needed to get addicted, as well as dependence on drugs, addiction. In this way, drug addiction progresses step by step. The same is the case with porn addicts.

Think about it, what happens to the sexual psychology of a person who is addicted to porn? Can a man who can't be aroused by watching hardcore pornography of a new woman or a child every day, have normal sex with a woman of real blood and flesh and sweat? So what does a man do when he reaches a climax, when he gets bored with rape videos or even child rape videos? What will excite him? Is he irritated by dissatisfaction, will he endure this intense hunger silently? You-I, we all know, intense sexual desire cannot be suppressed by mere "force of the mind". It can be done temporarily but it is not permanent. One time or another the explosion happens.

In fact, it does not work to release pornography; Rather, ab ... and leads the addicted person to perverted sex. As a result, the tendency of sexual abuse, child labor, rape and other perverted acts increases in the society. Much of which we have already discussed, you will find countless more proofs in the world around you. So much for sexual desire and sexual-psychological aspects. Apart from this, the theory of catharsis or any other theory of pornography being "useful" by the standards of common sense does not survive at all. If one watches videos of yaba or heroin food again and again, if these videos are presented in a glamorous way, will the use of yaba or heroin decrease in the society? Suppose you are told to reduce the rate of physical injury of children by teachers in primary schools in Bangladesh. Do you have these teachers as its solution Tell me, to watch the new videos of beating and torturing small children?

Would a video of young children being beaten and beaten in various ways and in different locations destroy their desire and mentality to be beaten? Would a person with a healthy brain take such a "solution" seriously at all? If the rate of rape decreases with watching porn, then why is there so much rape in America, the world's largest producer of porn and the largest consumer of pornography? Why is there so much rape, so much sexual harassment everywhere in the American military, college, Hollywood? Why is it that despite the popularity of rape in India, rape in India has not decreased but increased? Such self-serving propaganda is used to justify such harmful propaganda as "innocent entertainment." The same is true of masturbation. Most of the doctors, experts and internet websites of the present time will tell you that masturbation is not harmful at all.

He would like to prove that masturbation is "almost certainly" good for the body by bringing up evidence from various quarters. It's a very "natural" thing, there's nothing to worry about. Either good or normal sexual behavior such concrete 125/234 "normal", "natural" These words were introduced only seven-eight decades ago. Until then, masturbation, especially regular and chronic masturbation, was seen as an abnormal sexual act. Even whitewashing various sexual perversions, even perverted minded people like Sigmund Freud found masturbation unnatural.

The trend to view masturbation as normal and beneficial began in 1949 with the publication of Alfred Kinsey's Sexual Behavior in the Human Male. This book and his other book, Sexual Behavior in the Human Female, published in 1953, took the West by storm in direct collaboration with the mass media. It brings about a radical change in the Western view of sexuality. No other book or report on Western history has changed the West as much as these two books did. These two are the overall thinking of physicians about modern sex education, psychology and sex It is being run on the basis of books. The modern Western concept of sex is based on these two famous "theses" of Alfred Kinsey from beginning to end. In his book, Kinsey tries to perpetuate some of the most distorted thoughts in the name of science. She claims that babies are sexually active from birth, even in the womb. According to him, children start masturbating from a very young age.

Since childhood?

Kinsey claims that he has seen two-, four-, seven-month-olds, or a seven-month-old child capable of reaching orgasm through masturbation, and five other children under the age of one achieve orgasm on their own. / Can have pleasurable and beneficial sex with partners, and should. 231 Parents should masturbate children from the age of 6-7 years and masturbate together!

Kinsey further claims that most people are actually bisexual, with no specific criteria for sexuality. No sex is unusual. Homosexuality, bisexuality, childishness, bestiality, incest, whoever does what he wants, there is no problem.

In fact, Kinsey himself was a man of extreme perversion. Accustomed to horrible perverted sex in private life. His "research" was full of fraud. Later, the works of this "great" scientist have been proved wrong in the hands of scientists. Scientists have shown that Alfred Kinsey's claims have no scientific basis, and that his data is sufficiently convoluted. But by then the damage was done. "Masturbation is not harmful; Rather useful. "This extreme false claim of Kinsey's assertion has been repeatedly and credibly presented in the books of sex education and has been forced to be accepted as a constant truth. But if masturbation is normal and good, then why does a dark veil of remorse descend on the mind after the first masturbation?

After ejaculating through masturbation for the first time, almost everyone has extreme remorse. In such a situation of language, geographical location, religion and caste, people think that he has done something very bad. The feeling is universal. What is the explanation? "Experts" who want to prove that masturbation is good will say that religion and social values teach us to think that it is bad. It is a sin. And this is why remorse works in people.

Where is the mistake in this interpretation?

In order to be influenced by the statement of religion about a work, you have to know the work first, you have to know the statement of religion about it. But you will see that many people have no idea what is actually happening during the first ejaculation experience through masturbation. The boy who does not understand what happened, how will he know the religion's statement about the work, and will be affected by it? In fact, this is Fitrah, the natural disposition of man. The innate moral compass of man informs him that the work is bad. And so at first everyone suffers from remorse. But later people started to think it was normal.

In addition, real experience proves that masturbation addiction is not just a problem; Rather, it is a terrible psychological problem. We have already shared some of the experiences of the victims. Not one or two such tragic stories of masturbation addicts. Plenty.

Another big reason behind the rise of masturbation to normal evidence is the old calculus economy. Masturbation addiction and pornography are inextricably linked. These two together form a cycle. And hundreds of thousands of lives are trapped in this cycle. If masturbation is recognized as harmful, people are encouraged not to masturbate, counseling is given to stop masturbation addiction, what will happen to the hundreds of billions of dollars of pornography industry? Will the giant industry accept such a threat to its very existence? Or will he use his vast resources to try his best to prove that masturbation is normal and natural through academia, media and "experts"?

The next time you read Internet articles such as "Why Masturbation is Better", "17 Unknown Benefits of Masturbation", keep this in mind. Secondary, secondary evidence. The primary proof for us as Muslims is the statement of Islamic Sharia. And the statement of Islam is that masturbation is forbidden. 234 This should suffice as evidence for a Muslim. Where there is a clear provision of Islam, there is nothing to be taken for granted. Especially when the subject is related to morality. For example, in the eyes of science, extramarital sex is not harmful. Rather in modern Western philosophy it is normal, even admirable. On the other hand, in the eyes of Zina Islam, poets are sins. If science starts promoting zina as good for health from tomorrow, then it doesn't matter to a Muslim. This will not change his view of adultery.

So even if masturbation ever proves to be scientifically sound (which it hasn't yet), it shouldn't change a Muslim's point of view, because by Islamic standards it is immoral and haraam. And the reality is that psycho-physical masturbation and porn-addiction are both extremely harmful. We have already discussed how no one in the family and society has escaped its harmful effects.

The cycle of porn-addiction and masturbation traps a person's life in the quicksand of frustration, ugliness and repetition. After being trapped in this circle, hundreds of thousands of human souls began to decay. Breaking this cycle, what is the way out of this circle? Is it possible at all?

Out
Of
The Circle

It has been a while since the Asr prayers, the yellow sun has softened and started turning orange. The playground next to the mosque is full of orange sun. The mind became bored as I stared at the white grass blossoming on the green grass of the field. In a loud scream. The youngest son of the mosque attendant is trying to fly a kite in the field. Mr. Khadem is holding the red tuktuk kite, while the boy is running with the reed he is releasing the kite.

The red tuktuk kite is trying to float in the air with its nose up, but after a while it is diving and coming straight down to the ground. After several attempts, the red kite was finally able to fly, floating in the sky. Getting rid of any addiction is like flying a kite in the sky or learning to walk or cycling as a child. After falling many times, after stumbling, after many attempts, one can learn to ride a bicycle only, the kite's wings match in the sky. That's how you can't give up intoxication in one day, all at once - it will take time, it will take a lot of effort and strong morale.

Porn and masturbation complement each other. People watch porn

Masturbates and watches porn to masturbate again. Today's modern

The relationship between the two has become so inseparable in the world that it is not possible to solve the other without one. According to a peer-reviewed study, about 70 percent of men who masturbate at least once a week are severely addicted to pornography. 235 So your main focus in overcoming porn addiction should be to stay away from porn. Then it will be easier to stay away from masturbation and gossip

In sha Allah.

In this chapter, we will present to you some effective methods and tips to overcome porn and masturbation addiction. If these are followed sincerely, In sha Allah will be able to free himself from this cycle of porn-masturbation-chatir.

Litmus Test: How to understand if you are addicted to pornography

The prerequisite for solving any problem is to acknowledge the problem. The same is true of porn addiction. First of all you have to admit that you are addicted to porn, only then you will get the urge to get rid of the addiction from within. Even after being addicted to porn, if you still insist that you are not addicted to porn, you only occasionally watch a couple of porn videos, then there is no one to help you.

We are giving you 5 questions 238,238

Ask yourself these questions. If the answer to a question is "yes", then the alarm has gone off. You are addicted to pornography.

First question: Is the time spent watching your porn videos increasing day by day? Once you sit down to watch porn, you do not notice how much time has passed? Do you watch porn videos every day or every time longer than the day before? People who are addicted to pornography increase the amount of time they watch porn videos every day. It's like drug use. Once people start using drugs regularly, they discover that the dose that used to "work" is no longer there. Regular users therefore gradually increase the amount of drugs. Goes to find new porn videos. This search takes up a lot of time in their daily routine. This causes them to be late for school, college, varsity or work, feel lazy and do not feel cool working.

If you have these symptoms, you know that you are addicted to pornography.

The second question: Do you leave softcore porn videos and start watching hardcore porn

Did?

People addicted to pornography watch softcore porn videos in the first place. After a while, they lost interest in softcore porn. It doesn't seem "provocative" enough to them anymore. They look for something new and "tough". Slowly started watching hardcore porn videos. Thus they reach a point where incest, homosexuality or child rape videos provoke them, which seems normal to them. Disgusting things like oral sex and anal sex also become a nightmare for them.

If you are in this situation, you will understand that the alarm bell has rung — you are seriously addicted to pornography.

The third question: Do you have in your head the scenes seen in porn videos all day?

Stay?

After watching a porn video, it stays in the head of a porn-addict for a long time. The scenes seen in the video keep spinning in his head. While studying, working in the office, before going to bed at night, sitting idle, even while praying, his brain automatically starts thinking about the scenes of the last seen porn video. She compares the bodies of the women around her with the bodies of the heroines in the porn video, suffering from dissatisfaction with her wife's body (girls husband's body and her husband's performance in bed) and bed performance. She wants to have sex with her partner in the manner shown in the porn video. If the partner does not agree, he gets angry and upset. Complications are created about.

If you have any of these issues, you know you're addicted to pornography.

The same is true of porn addicts. After watching a porn video once or twice, they lost interest in it. There are three main tasks in a drug addict's routine. Raising money for drugs, buying drugs, getting intoxicated. His daily life, thoughts, plans and programs all revolve around these three. The same is true of porn addicts. The difference is that in this age of free internet pornography, porn addicts don't have to worry about money. Time for a porn-addict Q4: Do you feel depressed after watching porn videos? Is frustration consuming you day by day? Are you suffering from instability? Shame for your behavior? Does guilt work in you all the time? Good deeds create peace in the heart of people, create a feeling of intense love. Evil deeds, on the other hand, disturb the heart and make people feel guilty. If you feel depressed after watching a porn video, you will understand that it is an omen for you if you suffer from anxiety.

Question 5: Have you promised yourself or anyone else: I will never watch porn videos again, but you haven't kept that promise?

That is the most important question. People who are addicted to pornography promise themselves or anyone else that they will never watch porn videos again, but after a while or a few days they unknowingly forget that promise and go back to watching porn again. Many people stick another stick. Every time they watch a porn video, they make a firm commitment — this is the last time, I will never watch porn again in my life, I will not even come close to it. But after some time or a few days, they watch porn again and say this is my last time, I will never watch porn again.

Another important point is that many porn addicts say, "Damn! Why am I going to be addicted to pornography? I can leave it at any time I want. " But sadly, they can't stop watching porn videos if they want to.

Raise your hand ...

At the end of the day the fight is your own. We may give you shields and swords, your friend may give you armor and helmet, but you have to fight the duality of addiction.

Alone.

Can't you be like Moses (B)?

The thick water in front. There is no escape. Pharaoh's army is rushing back, furious. To cut Moses (a) and his (5) people to shreds. The eyes of Moses (3) say destruction is inevitable. Musa's (6) ears say destruction is inevitable. The argument is that destruction is inevitable. The people of Musa (as) are repeatedly asking Musa (25) "Where is your God? Where? "

Musa (Moses) disbelieved in his eyes, his ears, and did not pay heed to the words of his people. Contrary to the warnings of all the senses, he relied on the promise of Allah (swt). Believed. Introducing extreme tawakkul, he said, "Surely our Lord is with us. He will save us. "

This reward for relying on God (9) was given by God (9) to Moses (3) and by rescuing his people from the hands of Pharaoh and through the tomb of Pharaoh. Help came from Allah (1) from an unimaginable source.

"And whoever puts his trust in Allah, He is sufficient for him."

(Surat at-Talaq; 65: 3)

Brother, put your trust in God, fear Him. He is sufficient as a helper for His servants. He must arrange for you Do it, to overcome any danger, any adversity, any addiction.

The characteristic of a believer is tawakkul. God (69) says,

"Put your trust in God, if you are true believers."

(Surat al-Ma'ida; 5:23)

(Surah Tawbah; 9:51)

"And upon God let the believers rely."

Throughout the ages, believers have achieved something that is impossible from a natural point of view, incomprehensible to reason, through scientific formulas. It is not possible to explain accordingly.

The war with the Muslims is going on in the then superpower Persian Empire. Incredibly drawn superpower rates in several drawn wars. The Persians are running from Narsi to Madain for fear of defeat again. Saad Ibn Abi Waqqas (49), the commander of the Muslim army, is chasing after them. Following the chase of the Muslim forces, the Persian forces retreated and crossed the Tigris River. By the time the Muslim forces arrived on the banks of the river, the inferior fire-worshiping Persian forces had taken all the boats to the other side of the river. The Muslims had no way to get to the other side of the river. Every effort was made but no boat could be arranged. Finally, relying on Allah (19), they rode down the river on horseback. Many of the Muslim forces have never seen a river or a pond before. To them the huge Tigris River was like the Pacific Ocean.

Think about it, try to understand their psychology in that moment. If you were told to cross the ocean on horseback, would you ever agree? Finding no other way, they relied only on Allah () and went down to the river with their horses. The reward of tawakkul is given by Allah () proving all the sources of science wrong. Sader (1) forces crossed the river on horseback. When the Persian army saw the Muslims crossing the river on horseback, they thought they were not humans, but jinn. Frightened, they fled the battlefield. The Muslim forces got a taste of victory.

Tawakkul has two prerequisites. Without one the other is obsolete.

1. To have complete trust in Allah (19).

2. Try your best to use the means at your disposal.

Suppose you intend to recite Fajr in the mosque. He had full confidence in Allah that He would arrange for the Fajr prayers to be performed in the mosque. This was the first condition of Tawakkul.

Now the second condition is that you have to try yourself so that you can perform the Fajr prayers in the mosque, go to bed early, set an alarm if needed or talk about waking someone up. This is the second condition. In order to get the results of Tawakkul, you have to fulfill both these conditions. You relied on Allah (swt) but went to sleep after midnight, did not give alarm, did not ask anyone to wake up, sniffed at Fajr and went to sleep ... its name is not tawakkul. Allah (9) will not send angels to take you to the mosque on his lap.

You will do your job as much as possible, then Allah (19) will see the rest. That is Tawakkul. Doing everything you can, then relying on Allah (19) for success. Why did God tell Moses (9) to strike the sea with the stick in your hand? Why did God (9) then build a road under the sea? Musa (28) What can a small stick hit the vast sea like that?

By instructing Moses (ME) to hit the sea water, God (19) wanted to teach mankind that first you do your part, the rest I see. First you have to try your best. And Allah is the owner of success.

The God who made the road to the sea for Moses (69), the God who calmed the fire for Abraham (i), the moon that split the moon for Muhammad (), is the same God (9) is our God too! Can't that God (9) free us from these terrible addictions? Of course you can. But we are on him I don't get results without seeing Tawakkul or sincerely wanting to be free.

By God! By God! Only by relying on Allah (19) it is possible to get rid of any addiction including porn / masturbation / gossip. You have full faith in Allah (19) that He will arrange for you to be brought from this dark world to a world full of color, form, juice, smell and light. Then do as much as you can, honestly, sincerely. In sha Allah will see that any kind of addiction will not find the door to escape.

But just sitting there believing in Allah (4), not making any effort on your own, not looking down at girls, not stopping to see item songs, not stopping juicy conversations with friends about girls - then you will never get rid of addiction. No, never. God (9) is there to forgive you, waiting for you when you will return to Him. Raise your hand, He will pull you out of this filthy world and give you a place in Paradise.

Put your trust in your Lord, your Master. This time will soon be cut in sha Allah... ..

Break the circle

You have learned patience, mental fortitude and trust in Allah (74). Now it's your turn to go out in search of free air.

Sit in a secluded room with a pen and paper. Then dig out the memories and bring out the experiences right after masturbating, watching porn videos or reading short stories. Write down the details of how bad you feel after masturbating or watching porn videos, how many times you insult yourself, how many times you want to mingle with your soil. Why would you want to stop watching masturbation or pornography. Write everything one by one. Do not leave out the details. Find out why you masturbate or watch porn videos. Leave the papers carefully at the end of writing. These will be useful to us later.

Now sit down with a diary. Then write the year from which you started masturbating or watching porn and then write how many times a day you masturbated or how long you watched porn. The next line is for his next year. The next line is for his next year. Keep writing according to the serial till this year. Leave it well. Out of reach of children and parents, safely.

The next task is very important. Most people are about to do this show reluctance. You need to find a good friend. Maybe,that is your classmate, elder brother, a close relative or wife. To whom you mind you can talk openly and who is keeping your secrets secret keep it. Faithful. Tell him everything. This dark world that you repent want to get out of, say that. Want his help. Fight alone fighting in the combined strength of the two is much more appropriate than doing.If you are about 50 percent successful in overcoming porn / masturbation addiction In-shaAllah can do this. However, the opposite sex is mahram don't go to anyone again for help. Hit will be the opposite.

You have to delete all your porn videos. If you want to go to the internet and watch porn videos, you have to block porn sites. There are various apps and software for this. There is a detailed discussion in the article titled "Poison poisoning" (p. 209). Install these apps or software with the help of your trusted friend. Only your friend will know the password, you will not know. For this reason, even if you want to, you can no longer watch porn using your devices. Now it's time to set the target. If you masturbate every day, watch porn, then target yourself, from now on for the next 3 days I will not masturbate, I will not watch porn / I will not read gossip. Even if you can't meet the target, there is no problem. Set a three-day target again. If you can meet this target, set a new target, I will not masturbate for the next 7 days, I will not watch porn / read gossip. Set new targets again if you can meet it. I will not masturbate for the next 14 days ... keep going. And yes, don't forget to reward yourself every time you meet the target.

Feelings after watching a porn video or masturbating After waking up every morning on the piece of paper you wrote on, you will look at the paper once. If you feel like watching porn videos or masturbating, run and get those papers out of the secret place. Read carefully, thoughtfully. You are in a very critical situation now. Now if you lose to your instincts, the situation will be very bad. Most people understand that watching porn is bad, masturbating is harmful. But when he gets addicted to watching porn from inside, he fights with himself for a while, or I won't watch it ... but the fight doesn't last long. He surrenders to his instincts. Fight all your wills with one instinct.

And keep on invoking Allah (9). Remember over and over again how this addiction has deprived you of enjoying life! What a terrible loss! What a tragic outcome awaits you! Change places, get up while lying down. If you are sitting, get out of the house. Go somewhere where there is light, there are people, where there is warmth. Try to visualize, a poisonous snake is biting you on all sides. Fight with your whole being.

Sit down with that diary every week or two. Then write a report on your condition in a few days. To spend a month or two like this Then compare the current situation with the rate of masturbation in the previous years written in the diary, the time spent behind watching porn videos. In sha Allah you will see that there is a big difference. The rate of masturbation or viewing of porn videos has come down a lot - God willing (69) may have gone down a lot. If your condition does not improve after a month and a half, then it is a matter of concern. Maybe your intentions are flawed or you may not be able to focus properly or you may not be able to rely on Allah (74). Start applying the method we showed you from the beginning again and become a little more focused.

Take care of eye care, fast two days a week (Monday and Thursday), give alms. In sha Allah will work.

Trap

I saw a meme on Facebook. To Allah (1) in a small tax

Praying O God, give me patience. Give it right now, right now, not too late right now ... Patience is a very important factor in overcoming the addiction to porn / masturbation / gossip. But most of them have the same level of patience as that little one. If you want to overcome the addiction to porn masturbation-chat, you must be patient

Have to learn. In the end the fight must continue.

Allah (19) has informed us in the Qur'an that Satan is our open enemy. "Let him who follows in the footsteps of Satan know that Satan commands (seduces) obscene and evil deeds."

(Surah An-Noor; 24:21) "... I will lie in wait for them (the people) in your straight path. Then I will attack them (from all sides), from in front of them, from behind them, from their right side and from their left side. And you will not find most of them grateful. "

(Surat al-A'raf: 6: 16-17) Your enemy Satan is very patient and persevering. He will follow you with great patience. Will want to mislead with various tricks. One trap after another will continue to fall. You need more than luck to succeed in affiliate business. Otherwise the fall is inevitable.

In this article you will know some of the traps of the devil. With that you

It will be told how to cut the net and come out with your head held high.

One

Rajib kicked an empty bottle of cold drink lying on the concrete road and shook off both anger and resentment at the same time. "Dhuur! How long can you sit on a park bench with your stomach hungry? "

He has been sitting on this bench since that afternoon. It was getting late in the afternoon. Nothing has fallen into the stomach since Tiffin. On the front bench, the half-bedded man with broken hair and cheekbones was staring at Rajib in his school dress for a long time with his rat-like red eyes. Rajiv began to feel uncomfortable. That cannabis-eating guy can't help but snatch.

"Where's the ass! It is meant to be snatched from me, I don't even have a torn two taka note in my pocket ", Rajib thought to himself.

That's when the school holidays in the afternoon. But Rajiv is afraid to go home. He left for home several times and came back from the middle. Could not dare. When I go home today, my father will make him. The sun rises in the morning and sets in the evening, cows eat grass, these are the constant truth, just as it is a constant truth when you go home today and eat the lump in the hands of the father. Last week, while playing video games hidden in a school book, he was caught red-handed by his father yet his father did not say anything to him. He fled from home at noon the previous week and appeared on the sand field.

He had been playing cricket in the scorching sun like a hero and had been lying in bed for several days with a fever, but his father had not told him anything. But today there is no protection. Today he has given the result card of midterm and Rajiv is sitting in two subjects. Better a poor horse than no horse at all. On his forehead, Rajiv picked up the schoolbag from the bench and carried the empty water bottle on his shoulder. As much as he had learned Surah Qiraat from the master of Maktab in his childhood, he muttered and walked towards the house. ...

Please! God bless you today, I will pray from next Friday, I promised. Sure. Please God, please.

SubhanAllah! Human psychology is such that when a person is angry with someone else, he is afraid to go in front of him, he feels hesitant. Satan exploits this weakness of man to devise a plan to take the children of Adam away from his merciful and infinitely merciful Lord. You have fallen into the clutches of the devil and the nafs and have committed horrible sins — suppose you have watched porn videos or masturbated. After the tension subsided, you noticed, "Oh! Alas! What did I do? "

Burning in the fire of remorse, cursing himself. He immediately took a bath and stood in Jainamaya; The purpose is to repent. Arriving on the stage is the devil batter. He started whispering to you, "Kire hypocrite! A little while ago, disobeying God, now you have come to repent again? Share that! I see you have no shame, standing in front of God with a face? Do you think that God will forgive you? " You think, there is a lot of logic in the words. He began to suffer from dilemma, whether he would repent or not, forgetting how much Allah (s) and His Messenger (pbuh) encouraged repentance. The devil's plan is successful.

"Surely God loves those who repent to Him more and more, and He loves those who keep themselves pure."

(Surat al-Baqara, 2: 222)

"Those who do evil out of ignorance, then repent without delay, surely Allah will accept their repentance. Allah is All-Knowing, All-Wise."

(Surah An-Nisa; 4:16)

"Every son of Adam sins. The best of sinners are those who repent."

(Sunan Tirmidhi: 2499)

In Sahih Bukhari, Anas Ibn Malik narrates:

Allah's Apostle (*) said, "As much as one of you is happy to find a lost camel in the desert, Allah (69) is happier than him in the repentance of His servant."

(Sahih Bukhari: 5950)

Satan's plots cannot be ignored. Even if he calls you a hypocrite, he is actually a hypocrite. After committing any sin, repent immediately without delaying even a microsecond.

"O you who believe, repent to Allah with sincere repentance. It is not impossible that your Lord will forgive you your sins and admit you into Gardens beneath which rivers flow ..."

(Surah At-Tahrim; 6: 7)

What a wonderful way to screw people over.

"Stir hard, he will open the door for you, disappear, he will shine on you like the sun, fall down, he will take you to heaven, empty yourself, he will fill you with everything."

The devil's poor mind is very bad. Even after so many attempts, your repentance could not be stopped. Bouncer of his conspiracy, great hook sent you off the field. He understands why he wants to turn you away from repenting in this way, none of his fourteen ancestors. But he is not the one to give up so easily. Once again, a new trick has appeared on the stage - it will leave you with a whirlwind of repentance. Will play.

He started conspiring with you— "Watch the porn video first, then repent. Hey guy you don't know how much God is pleased if you repent? Forgive all sins? You also had fun and God was pleased, the snake died and the stick did not break! "

If a brother repents after committing a sin with such a plan, will repentance be accepted? Will God be pleased? You tell me to use the commonsense? It's a lot like that, you don't tell anyone on the street, you don't have a crow, you slap and punch happily, change the geography of your face, then say sorry, then will that poor thing ask you to wipe the blood from your smiling face, it's ok bro? Or brother-brother, mama-uncle-friend will call everyone and roll up their sleeves and rush towards you, "But Ray boy!"

Is it not possible to make a joke with Allah (4) by planning the deeds which Allah (9) has forbidden? And besides, watching porn If you die in a state of masturbation, you need to think about how you will be treated in the grave or on the Day of Judgment.

Be careful! When the devil starts giving such plots, he immediately seeks refuge with Allah (19) from the expelled devil. Turn off your laptop, phone (where you were preparing to watch porn videos) and leave. To the people. It is very good if you can perform ablution immediately and perform two rak'ats of prayer. It is better to call to prayer aloud; You know, when you hear the call to prayer, the devil runs away from the area with his life. Get away! Go away and die ...

Another of Satan's most effective tactics is "Today is the end. I will not watch porn videos or masturbate from tomorrow "- this thought is planted in your heart. Every tomorrow has another tomorrow; Tomorrow you will not think that today is the last time, who will guarantee it? It is an infinite loop with no end. You have to stop watching porn or masturbating today. If you can't do it today, there is no guarantee that you will be able to do it tomorrow.

Two

After becoming serious about Islam, the children of recent times began to suffer from a lot of romanticism about marriage. For some strange reason, they have made marriage the sole goal of their religious life and the main prerequisite for achieving their goals or objectives. Allah (9) knows the state of the heart well, but it seems so by looking at their outward behavior. The idea is that Islam only says to get married and not to do anything. They are very interested in "getting half of the religion" by getting married, but they are not so focused on fulfilling the remaining half of the religion.

With this marriage, the devil gets trapped in a very deadly trap, and our young people are so immersed in romanticism about marriage that they sit with their feet in that trap, and even if someone points a finger at them, they do not regain consciousness. For young people, marriage has become the solution to all problems.

"Why are you upset?"

"Because I Don't Have a Wife"

"Why is the result bad?"

"Because I don't have a wife, I'm upset, I can't read properly."

"Why is the Fajr prayer made up?"

"Because there is no wife, no one calls her with water in her mouth." "Why can't you stop watching porn videos?" Why do you masturbate? " "Because I don't have a wife."

Marriage is not a magic button that you press and all your problems will be solved. Some of the problems before marriage may go away after marriage, as well as many new problems will arise. Keeping an eye on each other, having a candle light dinner, riding a rickshaw together, eating phukka, these are not the only things that get married. Marriage means many responsibilities, many duties.

"It is not possible to get rid of porn-masturbation addiction before marriage, you can't give up even if you want to. The most effective way to get rid of porn-masturbation addiction is to get married, get married, everything will be fine, now forget the worries and go crazy.

Satan will swallow you up with so many lies. You will be disappointed. You do not want to be frustrated if you cannot get the right pitch so invest in a good capo. Your thoughts will revolve around marriage. But at the present time marriage has been made very difficult. It will be seen again that even if you think about marriage all day long, you are not taking any concrete steps to get married. Not making a living. Maturity is not coming in behavior. There is no impression of responsibility in the work. Far from explaining to his family, he may not be able to start a conversation with them. But day and night constantly thinking about marriage is not stopping.

It will take a long time to see your parents talking about marriage. Even after burning a lot of wood, you may not get married when you want. You will become more frustrated. Watching porn, masturbating will continue to increase. Life will seem unbearable. But if you follow the other tips, then maybe you will get rid of porn-masturbation addiction.

If you think that you will get rid of porn-masturbation addiction just by getting married, you will make a serious mistake. You may be able to stay away from these for a while, but then whoever. Too many married brothers horrible kind of porn You are addicted to masturbation. Porn-addiction has broken down the homes of many. Porn addiction is responsible for 56 percent of divorces in the United States. Fifty-five percent of married American men admit that they watch porn videos at least once a month. 239 25 percent of married American women admit that they watch porn videos at least once a month. And 18 percent of unmarried American women who watch porn at least once a month. 240

But why marriage is not the complete solution to porn or masturbation?

Porn-addiction will change the structure of your brain. We have discussed this in detail in the first part of the book. You will lose interest in real sex. With the ability to have sex. Your wife can't prepare you for sex, you will find it provocative and satisfying to sit in a corner of the house and watch porn instead of being intimate with her. After marriage, you will understand the exaggerated idea that was born in you about the body of a woman by watching porn. You will be disappointed. The brain programmed by your porn will be more attracted to the plump bodies of porn actresses than your wife. You will go back to the world of porn.

The whole point of intimacy is to get close to two people very nicely, which is really a blessing from Allah (19). Satisfying the wife or husband because of love and affection. Thinking more of his wife's satisfaction than of himself; Ensuring that the whole time is comfortable for him, that he does not suffer or be treated indiscriminately, that he is respected.

The whole point of porn goes against intimacy, because the main thing here is taking and selfishness. Give yourself pleasure until you are satisfied, keep looking for something new. Because you are addicted to porn, you do not pay attention to what your wife wants. Unsatisfied with the normal way, you will lean towards anal sex, oral sex, will insist on the wife. If the wife does not agree, you will remain dissatisfied. Will start watching porn again. Apart from that, the amount of sexual satisfaction in anal sex, oral sex decreases.

You will be dissatisfied even if you get the chance of these. You have to masturbate after watching that porn.

After marriage, husband and wife like each other. The two are constantly discovering and fascinated by each other. The storm of love. But after a while, especially after a loop of 10 years, the storm of love stopped. The pull of the heart, Maya-Mamta is the same as before, but physically your wife may not pull you like before. He may not be able to give you as much "quality time" as he used to. Maybe that's why you suffer from boredom with sex. But in an institution called marriage, sex is not everything; Rather it is one of the many parts of marriage. Interdependence, trust, love, sense of responsibility are also part of marriage. So the problem that all men will or will suffer from monotony in sex life with age is how porn affects the thoughts of fifteen. Porn will not let you be satisfied with a partner.

It is very difficult for those who are accustomed to watching porn to be satisfied with a sexual partner. The characteristic of porn is to create monotony about normal sex. Even a porn-addict may find the same type of porn boring at times. He needs something tougher. From softcore to hardcore, from hardcore to rape porn, gay porn, child porn thus continues to be her "improvement". In the blue world, the woman of blood and flesh, who is always intoxicated by the new apsaras, will get old very quickly and will look pale. The monotony of sex will show you the way to porn and masturbation. Hundreds of thousands of people have been freed from the addiction of porn-masturbation without marriage. You can too in sha Allah. Keep relying on Allah (19) and keep trying, as well as make yourself worthy for marriage. I can't get married so I can't save myself from porn-masturbation addiction, don't give these excuses.

Three

Life is unbearable due to porn-masturbation addiction. You want to get rid of these. After drinking Adajal, he clung to his waist, determined mind. Everything is going well. It's been a long time but you haven't even come close to porn-masturbation. Very happy, he breathed a sigh of relief - let the father live Gone ... But one day there was a breakdown in a hurry watching porn videos or masturbating. After it was cold, he started tearing his hair with regret - alas! Alas! What did I do! At such a time, Iblis appeared on the stage to sprinkle salt on Katagha. No matter how hard you try, you can't get rid of porn-masturbation addiction. I followed so many tips, I did so many things, could I survive from these? Exclude these nonsense ... "He will continue to give such conspiracies until you stop trying to get rid of porn-masturbation addiction out of frustration.

There is nothing to despair about. Porn-addiction is almost as horrible as cocaine addiction. One day, it will not be possible to intercept pornography or masturbation addiction for the rest of one's life, it will take some time. Don't be discouraged. Repeatedly defeated in the battle of masturbation, porn-addiction does not mean "losing". You will be defeated on the day you give up trying to escape from the devil's temptation to masturbate, porn-addiction.

Never give up. Be patient, rely on Allah (19). In sha Allah you will be victorious. In sha Allah one day the bright yellow sun will rise all around, the leaves of the trees will sway in the breeze, the dove will whistle sweetly, you will be freed from the prison of masturbation, porn-addiction and you will fly in that beautiful blue sky in that open air. On that day all your frustrations, troubles, anxieties, sorrows will come together in grief and apologize that they were utter liars.

Four

As soon as he woke up and opened the door and came to the verandah of the hall, his heart became "happy". The sun is shining brightly all around. The sky is very blue. It was as if someone had poured blue all over the sky. How unbearably beautiful!

The pair of storks are catching insects in the grass with their yellow legs. The grass is like a green carpet. The white grass flowers are trembling in the gentle wind. In the forest of coconuts, mangoes, blackberries and jackfruits a sigh of relief rose. The mango branches are swaying, clapping their hands as if to the ventricles; Income ventricle, income ...

Nilay did not understand what to do after breakfast. Today is a holiday. No problem with class or lab. I was wondering if I would be able to sleep again. There is no benefit in sleeping. I watch a movie more than that. I don't know if a new Bengali movie has come out.

Niloy started watching movies on YouTube. Conventional story. After a while a song started. Item No. Nilay is a polite boy. Sometimes he goes to the mosque except on Fridays. I was ashamed to see the kandakarkhana of the item. The whole thing skipped. After a while another song started. Even if the item is not sung, it is quite obscene. This time he saw the whole thing for a while. Someone said to him from inside, "Look, boy, once you see it, nothing happens."

When he finished watching the whole movie, his condition was very bad. The ears are hot. The heartbeat has increased too much. Breathing loudly. Twenty-two springs have passed and the thirsty body has awakened. Turning the ventricle, Santa saw the item several times (he looked down in embarrassment the first time he saw it) several times. Then one by one he saw several. From within, he was repeatedly forbidding the existence of a good man. He did not pay attention to it at once. Tensions continued to rise. At one time Nilay did the heinous act. After cooling down, he regained consciousness. Deep exhaustion engulfed him. The world that used to look so beautiful in the golden sun a little while ago, wanted to thank Allah (69) again and again, now looks very damp, dark.

Wanting to die. Nilay does not know how many times he has to be defeated by his nafs and Satan. In this way, Iblis has been deceiving their children from time immemorial, from time immemorial, from Adam (a) and Eve (a). She will never tell you directly, "watch porn" or "masturbate". He will proceed step by step with great patience. He will make the first step very interesting to you. He will come up with a lot of logic to do the job. Just as Adam () and Eve (b) were deceived. We all know the incident. God (9) forbade Adam (I) and Eve (not) to eat the fruit of a tree. He even forbade her to go near the tree. But Satan left them eating the fruit of that tree. Satan did not tell them at first, "You eat the fruit of this forbidden tree." Satan first to Adam (8) and Eve (3) He went and said, "Look! I am your friend, I want to benefit you.

If you eat the fruit of this tree, you will live forever. You can live in this paradise forever. " They were deceived by the devil and disobeyed the command of Allah (19) and ate the fruit. The beginning of the journey of the children of Adam from this paradise to the world full of misery that's it.

The Barsisa incident in Israel is another classic example of Satan's step-by-step deception. Satan slowly deceives Barsisa, who is very worshipful, and makes her fall in love with a young woman. Then he committed adultery with her. When the girl is pregnant, Iblis persuades Barsisa to kill him. Finally, he forced Barsisa to prostrate to the devil.

He will set a similar trap to overwhelm you. The first step will be a seemingly very simple, innocuous thing. Looking at girls on the street, watching movies occasionally, watching a little video on YouTube, following a girl on Facebook, liking a profile picture, chatting occasionally, or chatting with "like sister" / "just friend" girlfriends, hanging out, etc. . If you make up your mind to do these things, he will make a thousand arguments in front of you; Hey one day ..., sometimes you need a little entertainment! Is Islam so strict? I'm just chatting, I'm not in love anymore ... What will happen if I see a girl; Allah (4) is such a beautiful creation, why not see Ma Sha Allah? We are not like that, even if we sit together and chat, even if we sit in the same rickshaw, nothing bad comes to our mind — we are just friends ... thousands of such arguments.

If the devil's leaf falls into this trap once, then you are trapped. There is a good chance that you will be sucked into the devil's hands and book a hell of a hole for yourself. You can think because of the extra self-confidence, hey shit! You are frightening me unnecessarily ... Satan will never be able to feed me, on the contrary, I will make him run. That's the first step, then I'm not going. Like you, Barsisa thought, "Until that first step. Then I will not go any further. " But once he walked all the steps of the first, second and third steps, he committed a heinous sin like prostrating to the devil. That won't happen to you either What is the guarantee. Barsisa was a very great worshiper (Abid). But in the end it had such a tragic consequence — I, you, no ashes.

Besides, Allah (9) forbids us to tempt ourselves. But he did not say do not commit adultery, he said do not go to adultery.

So, being confident, with the idea of damn care, you get rid of all these temptations there is no point in throwing in. Confidence is good, but extra only fools have confidence. Many more places to paint you get it, it's better not to do it here. This is the question of Paradise-Hell. The reality try to understand. You know very well what things are throws you into fitnah. Which triggers little by little you running to watch porn, masturbate or commit real adultery. She list the topics. It is written on the back of the truck, you have not seen 6100 hands stay away? In the same way, rushing towards adultery is 100 hands from those things stay away. Do not even approach. Do not give the devil any chance.

Do not accept any argument.

Five

It's not too late to finish graduation. Once upon a time, the only goal and purpose of life was to get a good job and marry someone of your choice. Now when I think of the job, my body becomes confident. Exclude jobs. Do business, business. Leaving the fan at full speed with the kantha on before going to sleep I think of business. I'll start a business in the town of Mooseball with a little money, then the business will slowly flourish. The headquarters will be in that mooseball city, but branches will be opened in all major cities of the country including Dhaka. There will be cars, there will be houses, there will be wives. Cox's Bazar once a month, tours abroad at least once a year. When my eyes become sleepy thinking about this happy day in the future! Bhagyas did not tear my thorn; Otherwise, the critics would sit with their faces bent, dreaming of lakhs of rupees lying on torn rags!

Have we ever considered that being able to think, dreaming of the future is a great blessing of Allah (9)? What deeply people can think! What a wide range of his thoughts! What a clumsy, uninteresting book he has written just thinking! Has changed the course of the world!

Subhan Allah !!

It is very important to control your thinking. In most cases, pornography / masturbation / gossip starts with unbridled thinking. Before going to bed at night or in a lazy moment, I thought of a girl or a scene seen in a porn video. You started thinking about that girl or the scene. Your thoughts became increasingly dangerous. Awaken your inner instincts. It created pressure to do those heinous things. One day you will bow to that pressure, surrender to Satan.

So be careful about thinking. The devil's most powerful tool for your downfall is uncontrolled, unbridled thinking. Again, this is a very powerful tool. It will be much easier to get rid of your addiction if you can disable this tool of the devil. There is joy in thinking badly about a girl or in fantasies about porn actresses, there is momentary fun. But the end result is terrible; Lelihan flames of hell.

What you can do:

1) I have fun thinking for a while, I will not think later, such a mentality can not exist. As soon as bad thoughts arise, one should seek refuge in Allah (19). The stalks of thought cannot be

allowed to grow. You need to shift the focus of your thinking, talk to people, change places, or get busy.

2) There are some girls who, as soon as you think about it, you feel a pressure to watch porn or masturbate. As soon as you think of these girls, you will seek refuge with Allah (19) and also pray for those girls, so that Allah (19) may guide them, heal the wounds of their hearts and give them the tawfiq of living a holy life. Thus Praying is very effective. This will change your outlook. Those girls are no longer just for you to enjoy; Rather, he is a living being of flesh and blood with all human feelings of happiness, sorrow, laughter and tears. Wanting to love them too, wanting to be loved, wanting to dream, wanting to see the moon with your head on the shoulder of your loved one, you are remembering the name of Allah (9), praying to Him. At this time Satan will not be able to take advantage of much. Your focus will change.

And if Allah (69) guides someone because of your prayers, then it is a matter of wondering what a great reward awaits you.

3) It is necessary to make arrangements so that bad thoughts do not come. Just friend, just friend game, holy love, holy love game must stop.

"We are just friends, our minds are pure, there is no sin in our minds, we are like brothers and sisters", please do not make such ridiculous claims. Why are you acting like this? Why are you fooling yourself? You know, I know what you're saying is a lie. You haven't fantasized about your "just friends", you haven't talked to other friends about them, you haven't masturbated thinking about them. Don't tell these lies. Where it is haraam to look at girls, there is no question of making love, making friends with them.

Free association with girls also turns men into sexual mode. When a man interacts with a woman, his body secretes testosterone, which prepares him for the ultimate intimacy with that woman. And if testosterone secretion levels are too high, the person feels the need to be intimate. You can't be intimate with your "just friend" at that very moment, so go to the bathroom and cool yourself, right?

Please close these. It is very difficult to come back from the addiction of porn / masturbation / gossip. It becomes more difficult, even impossible, for you to return to these tasks.

4) Make veil with all the women except mahram. Even with close relatives. A mahram is a person whom it is haraam to marry. For example: grandmother, grandmother, mother, step-mother, aunt, uncle, sister, step-sister, mother-in-law, daughter, granddaughter, brother's daughter, sister's daughter, son's wife is mahram for boys. It is permissible to marry any woman other than a mahram, that is, a non-mahram woman. Bhabi, aunt, uncle, sister-in-law, cousin (cousin, cousin, cousin) are all mahram in Gair. You have to screen with them

If you want to get rid of the addiction of porn, especially chatigalpa, you must screen with them. Otherwise, your conversations with them, your movements, your conversations will remind you of gossip or incest porn. The resistance you have developed against gossip or porn will be shattered. You go back and forth to chat or porn. Satan always deceives people with these relationships.

So there is a good risk of making a mistake (God forbid). Apart from that, because of reading gossip or watching porn, you have a bad thought about them all the time, you keep it down with great difficulty. Interacting with them, that thought will swell in conversation, how long will it take for the explosion to happen?

Maximum effort must be made to comply with the screen. If this is not possible, try to minimize the interaction. Cousins, sisters-in-law, sisters-in-law, when a girl classmate comes to tell a story, stay sullen, yes, get the job done. You will see that they will gradually move away. The best technique is to become a "master". Leave the beard, start wearing a hat on your head, try to lower your eyes whenever you see a mahram woman in Gair, you will see that your cousin or sister-in-law is not coming to chat with you, I think you are going away with a cloth on your head. Even though it is important to do these things, if you have not done so, at least do it with this help.

At first you may think that if you stay away from the mahram women like Qazin, Bhabi or other guys, they will think you are anti-social. Think you're loose. You will understand later that it is right On the contrary, they will respect you a lot because you are so far away. If you give an example of a good boy, your name will come to mind first.

5) The most important thing is to take care of the eyes. The Prophet (peace be upon him) said, "The eye is the arrow of Satan." Only with the care of these eyes can you save yourself from porn-masturbation addiction, and your life will change. Try eye care for a week. You will feel the difference yourself.

The Messenger of Allah () said,

"The human body has a body of flesh that, if it is right, the whole body is right; And if it is destroyed then the whole body is destroyed. And that is the club or the heart. "

(Bukhari: 52; Muslim: 417) If the club or heart is right, all the deeds of faith will be right, and if the club is defiled, the twelve acts of faith and deeds will be sounded. Satan wants to take control of your heart in the first place, so that you can turn your nose around at will. The sight of the eyes is the trump card of the devil. Through this he can easily take possession of your heart. And once you take possession of the heart, he will make you do whatever sin he wants.

Is it possible to take care of the eyes at all in this sexual tickling society?

Yes, difficult but possible. When walking on the road, you have to walk looking at the ground, you can't stand on the sidewalk of the girls school, you can't hang out. Places where girls are more likely to be anagona or where free mixing is more likely to be abandoned.

The Companions (9), the Tabi'is and the pious people of the previous age need to know about eye care. They have to be taken as competitors; If they can, why can't I ...

Movies, dramas, music must be avoided, the entertainment page of the magazine should be carefully avoided. A very effective way is to keep track of how many times a day you have not been able to take care of your eyes. Then as an expiation, perform two rak'ats of nafl prayer for each time. Suppose, if you have not been able to take care of your eyes a total of 10 times a day, then perform a total of 20 rak'ats of Nafl Salat for these 10 times. Keep doing it this way.

You have not been able to take care of your eyes after being deceived by the devil, but when the devil sees you praying two rak'ats every time you do not take care of your eyes, he will regret it. He will help you to take care of your eyes in order to deprive you of the reward of Nafl Salat.

After listening to these tips for praying, a very good feeling works in my mind, "Let's go, Dad! And it will not be a problem to take care of the eyes. " But sadly, these tips are hard to follow. You looked at the girls as you wished all day, drank the beauty, thinking, "I will perform the prayer at night as an expiation," but in the end you will see that the prayer will no longer be performed. If there is no sincerity about Amal, eye care will not be done anymore. So you have to make a strict promise that even if you pray 100 rak'ats, you will perform 100 rak'ats.

YouTube is another notable way to watch porn videos and masturbate. You have no bad intentions in mind, just sit on YouTube to watch a good video, then keep peeking at some videos in the suggestion list. Even if you don't want to look that way, sometimes the eyes will go away. And then the devil will come and catch you. And don't say that you only sit for 10 minutes watching videos on YouTube. Once you sit on YouTube, one and a half hours go by in any direction, you don't even know. Just a waste of time. If you had a little more intimacy at this time, your CGPA would have been healthier, you would have gotten a better job, and the father of a beautiful girl might have lost his mind in the future.

Many times, of course, there is no way. You have to sit on YouTube to watch a tutorial or listen to a good lecture. There will be suggestions Start browsing by saying Bismillah. It is better if K9 is installed. You can't access nonsense videos even if you want to.

In your spare time, never sit on YouTube and watch random videos (read the sentence a few times, stick it in your head). The devil plots too much in his spare time. You will find a more detailed discussion of how to escape the trap of YouTube in the article "Poison poisoning".

Six

Another effective trap of the devil to get used to masturbation is nightmares. He will tell you, "Look, nightmares are very annoying. If it is winter, there is no word. Midnight sleepy eyes, trousers, blankets, blankets, wet, sticky, sticky liquid. In the body. Heat the water, pull the bucket, hide the parents, brothers and sisters and take a very careful bath. What a shame! Even if the parents look a little differently, it is doubtful, this is understood! Suppose you went to visit a relative's house. Your nightmare at night is how troublesome it is to get up in the morning and take a bath in front of a crowd of people! Without it, nightmares are very harmful for the body. Instead, you should masturbate once a week. Then you don't have to worry about nightmares anymore. "

I have a lot of friends who don't just masturbate, but just masturbate at regular intervals to avoid nightmares. Satan deceived them.

We need to discuss nightmares in a little detail.

After getting a little older, everyone manages more or less, but in adolescence or early youth, nightmares are a very scary experience. It is normal for a ten- to twelve-year-old boy to panic when he wakes up one night and sees his pants soaked in sticky liquid. To unravel the mystery of this sudden change of body, he seeks refuge with friends, neighbors, cousins or his own siblings. She does not forget to discuss her physical changes with her parents or other elders. Some shame and the rest because of the generation gap. In our society about nightmares Due to the prevailing superstitions, fake doctors, violence of herbal companies, lack of accurate information, a small brain is burdened with misinformation. He panics even more. Physical and mental development is severely hampered.

But the Muslims were not supposed to be like this. Unnecessary shame and luxury do not suit Muslims. The female companions (9) have asked Rasulullah himself (*) about the nightmare, "O Rasulullah ()! Allah (14) is not ashamed to reveal the truth, if a woman has nightmares, should she take a bath? "

The thought is that we have become more shy than Rasulullah (7) and his Companions (9)! We know more manners than them! Alas! We should talk openly about these matters. That doesn't mean, "I had nightmares!" Saying this, I will beat the drum in the market. With a little effort, the correct information can be conveyed to everyone by maintaining decency and eliminating the confusion of nightmares very effectively. We can use the mosques.

Imam Sahib or a young scholar one day invited all the rising boys of the mahalla to the mosque. Some food and drink, gossip. In between, there was a discussion about porn, the disadvantages of masturbation, the importance of eye care, nightmares, the importance of achieving holiness and methods. If you search, you will find many doctors who will participate in such programs with great interest. With a little sincerity and goodwill, our teenagers will be able to acquire this vital knowledge from the purest people in the society.

There is no need to spend a lot of money on sex education, no need to give a chance to people like Alfred Kinsey and John Money to implement the agenda with the help of foreign NGOs. Ensuring quality sex education is possible with very little logistical support and low budget. By God! Our mosques are deserted today. There is no dars of Quran, there is no halaqa of Hadith. People like robots pray with sijdah, then come out. The members of the mosque committee do not have any problem with these. All their headaches are installing AC in the mosque, installing tiles With Where are we as a nation? Young people in the mosque are afraid to sit with the Quran! Afraid to lighten up! Khatibs are afraid to talk about religion, the Messenger of God ()!

Anyway, let's get to the real thing, leaving out the patch of regret.

What is nightmare?

The nightmare is the semen coming out of the genitals spontaneously by dreaming of intimacy between men and women in their sleep.

Nightmares usually occur at night. This is why it is called Nocturnal Emissions Academically. However, sometimes there are nightmares during the day. 250 All men go through this experience at least once in their lives. According to Islamic Sharia, nightmares are one of the signs of a boy becoming an adult. A child will be considered an adult from the time of the first nightmare and the Shariah will apply to him. 251.

Nightmares usually start from the age of 12-13 years. Just as boys have nightmares, girls also have nightmares.

Why is nightmare?

This question is difficult to answer. It is not possible to say exactly what causes nightmares.

Nightmares begin during adolescence, when the male body begins to produce the hormone testosterone 52. Under the influence of this hormone, men behave masculinely, men and women feel physical attraction towards each other. The hormone testosterone helps in the production of semen. When the amount of testosterone is higher than normal, the old semen comes out through nightmares Goes and new semen is made. Prolonged sexual inactivity is another possible cause of nightmares. Sexual inactivity increases the amount of testosterone, which causes nightmares.

Excessive fatigue, sleeping after tight clothing, sleeping late and late

Waking up, waking up in the morning and sleeping again, sex all the time

Being stuck in fantasy — these are also possible causes of nightmares.

How many days after the nightmare?

There is no way to say for sure. Some people have nightmares after one week, while others have nightmares after three or four weeks.

Is nightmare harmful?

There is a lot of misleading talk about this in our society. Nightmares are a completely natural thing. It is not harmful to the body at all.

Allah (e) has forbidden only those things which are harmful to man. For example, alcohol, marijuana. Allah (69) has forbidden these to save people from harm. Nightmares are a completely natural thing. It is not forbidden by Allah (9); Rather, he has made it a sign of adulthood. The Qur'an says:

"And when your children grow up (through nightmares) ....

(Surah Noor; 24:59)

Narrated Ali: The Prophet (peace and blessings of Allaah be upon him) said:

"Withdrawal of pen from the record of three persons 1) Until the sleeping person wakes up

2) Until the children become adults 3) Until they become insane. "

(Tirmidhi: 1343; Ibn Majah: 3032; An Nasai: 337)

A sleeping person does not even know what he is doing in his sleep. Then his deeds are not recorded. Nightmares occur while asleep and are also not recorded in the diary. 254 If nightmares were harmful, then Allah (9) would have forbidden it and used to arrange punishment for nightmares. None of them (19) didn't. So we Muslims can believe with our eyes closed there is no harm in dreaming. According to the doctors, nightmares also occur not harmful.

It is halal to drink water. But if you continue to drink glass after glass of water, then it is definitely not good. Excessive nightmares are also not good. If you have frequent nightmares for a long time, say you have nightmares every day or two, then you can consult a specialist. I repeat, specialist physician. Not a fake doctor.

Don't listen to the devil when he comes to plot against you. Have nightmares, but don't forget to masturbate to avoid nightmares.

Seven

The test trap is a terrible trap. Especially for airy, dodgy students. As such, there is tension in the head during the exam, and there is a lot of pressure on him if he stays away from studies throughout the year. Unable to cope with this pressure, many people watch porn or masturbate. As we have seen with countless young people, their levels of viewing porn or masturbating during the test season increase dramatically. Again, many people become addicted to watching porn or masturbating during exams. Leads to frustration, leads to instability.

Student life is a wonderful time. Every moment of it should be enjoyed. My brother, why are you making life miserable by sitting alone in a dark room watching porn and masturbating in frustration and instability? Get out of the room a little. See what a beautiful world awaits you. Hang out with friends, go for walks in groups, walk barefoot on the green grass, lie down and watch the sky, get wet in the rain, play sports on the field, go cycling, run. If you feel very frustrated, go to the mosque if you are upset. Pick up a copy of the Quran from the shelf. Start reading any page, you will see frustration, where the bad will run away!

Even if you just sit in the mosque, you will see that your mind will get better.

You have to sit with books all day, you have to study, I'm not saying that. Keep an ear open to the occasional lecture while Facebooking in class. If you want, keep it in the lecture book from time to time. Keep an eye on the topics before a weekend day or class test. Go to the friend you read the night before the exam, go to the weekends instead of the night before the exam. These little things will keep you going. The test will no longer be stressful. You don't even have to work inhumanely. Disappointment will not come, God willing. You don't have to watch porn or masturbate to relax the excited nerves.

Eight

Facebook is like a knife. If the knife is in the hand of the doctor, it saves life, if it is in the hand of the painter, it takes the life. Facebook is the same. If you can use it well, Facebook will change the course of your life. And if you are a little careless, life will be ruined. Facebook was not like that once, the competition of knowledge, the competition of beauty, the competition of showing happiness in married life, the competition of showing power, there was no exhibition of one's personal, family, social life on Facebook.

Imagine for a second you were transposed into the karmic driven world of Earl. Looking at the selfies of friends in expensive restaurants, looking at pictures of traveling abroad, you have become restless, restless. When your friends on Facebook are arranging the imaginary happiness and success of their lives, your heart is poisoned, envious. The algae of despair has accumulated in your mind. One sigh after another ... "Damn it! Nothing happened in life! " The moss of despair has become thicker, has become more green. How many times the devil has given you so many moments in this moment of despair Got it. You've watched porn, masturbated, and finally shed tears of regret.

As much as you can, spend less time on Facebook. However, if you are not forced to leave at once. Moderate Facebooking is a very useful thing in many cases. Follow the Islamic pages, those who do not mix truth with falsehood or follow the right-wing scholars who do not interpret Islam in the Western way. Facebook can help you a lot in these aspects.

Unfriend your friends who share pornographic pictures, videos, etc. If you don't want to unfriend, unfollow. Placing the cursor on the ID unfollows the following text. This ID will be in your friend list but will not show in the news feed. It did not offend the eyes, nor did the friend get angry. In the middle you survived the fitnah. You can use a browser extension called facebook purity to remove the IDs to follow different models, ads on different pornographic pages, etc. on the right side of Facebook. Firefox, chrome for both browsers.

There are many pages on Facebook that spread pornography. These pages cannot be followed in any way. Can't follow heroine, actress, model or any celebrity. You need to keep your homepage clean. No girl's picture should come. Even if you see a picture of a girl while scrolling through Facebook, it can trigger you to watch porn or masturbate. So our suggestion is not to have any other girl in your friend list except mahram. There are many brothers who drink ginger water to get rid of porn and masturbation.

But because of being trapped in the net of women's sedition on Facebook, porn and masturbation are no longer possible. Today, unfriend everyone of the opposite sex right now. Cousins too. (If you don't want to unfriend the cousins, you can unfollow them, but we will strongly discourage them. Unfriend straight away. You may have to listen to some difficult things, but in the end you will benefit from it in sha Allah)

Finding out all the girls / boys in the friend list and unfriending them is a hassle and time consuming matter. But there is an easy solution.

For Boys

If you follow the link below, you will find those who have gender females in your friend list

All IDs will come in sha Allah. Then you can easily unfriend them.
https://www.facebook.com/search/females/me/friends/interse ct

The problem with the link above is that use this link:

https://m.facebook.com/search/females/me/friends/intersect

For Girls:

If you go to the link below, all the IDs of the gender mailed IDs in your friend list will come in In sha Allah. Then unfriends them

You can do very easily.
https://www.facebook.com/search/males/me/friends/intersect

If there is a problem with the link above:

https://m.facebook.com/search/males/me/friends/intersect

Never interact with someone of the opposite sex on Facebook. Never chat. The brothers practicing Islam also fell into this trap. No need to answer even if a girl asks you something in the inbox. Needless to say, you don't want to reply for fear of fitnah. Satan will try to deceive you again and again. It will remind you of the importance and virtue of medicine. Do not forget the deception of the devil. Comment, when you go to invite Deen in the inbox, you will not even know when you will be sitting with the invitation of the heart.

I would request you to please reduce the amount of photo uploads on Facebook. Why don't you understand that taking selfies while sitting up and uploading them on Facebook is a kind of illness, mental imbalance? By uploading photo after photo on Facebook, what is the benefit to you in flying the lantern of happiness with all the imaginary statuses? How much because of you People's hearts are being poisoned! It's about creating tension. At the same time, you are being harmed by "eye 256"!

Everyone is annoyed that you keep uploading selfies, but for the sake of politeness, no one says why don't you understand? My sisters, why don't you understand, the boys who made appreciative comments on your pictures suffer in fantasy with you? Have ugly discussions with you about their friends? Do you really want to be the heroine of the sexual fantasy and masturbation of a boy with perverted taste? I don't understand, I don't understand why you insult yourself like this!

Some fraudsters collect pictures of girls from Facebook, then edit them and post them on porn sites or chat pages, often blackmailing them. This also needs to be kept in mind.

No,

The Devil's Leaf Another deadly trap is modern boyfriend / girlfriend culture. The devil gets into a very deadly trap with his girlfriend. One of the tips we used to get rid of porn and masturbation was to tell a close friend about it and ask for help. Satan will tell you, "Hey crazy, who is closer to you than your girlfriend? Share everything with him. Isn't he an iconic inspiration for you? Looking into his eyes, holding his hand in your fist, do you not feel the power of world conquest in yourself? Without it, the rebellious poet says,

'Never was the sword of a victorious man alone

You can say goodbye to porn and masturbation addiction only with the inspiration of Vijay Lakshi Nari's girlfriend.

Love itself is a deadly fitnah. To disobey the command of Allah step by step. By talking to your girlfriend, by looking at her, by dating, by touching you, you are disobeying the command of Allah . Doing so and giving the devil a chance to take control of your heart. He is taking control of your heart and making you do whatever you want.

You are watching porn.

Masturbating.

There is no reason to think that love is a panacea for masturbation / porn addiction. Love may keep you away from porn-masturbation for a very short time, but it will not provide any solution in the long run. No matter how "sacred" (?) That love is. What do most boys do? Tell yourself.

He also loves to watch porn videos and masturbate again. This haraam relationship can take you to Liton's flat or "room date" at the end of the hooded rickshaw, KFC, light-dark restaurant, Star Cineplex episode. And that must be worse than porn and masturbation.

Ten

If you want to get rid of your addiction to porn / masturbation / chat stories, you have to say goodbye to all the friends who are addicted to it themselves. If you continue to interact with them, it will be difficult to get out of addiction. They will invite you to watch porn, "Come on dude, let's see today ...", "There is a new collection. Let's see ... "

Maybe - or sitting and chatting. Someone hurriedly started chatting or porn video story, started juicy talk about girls. Even if you don't join their discussion, some obscene terms, some words will stick in your head. Later when your brain is lazy, when you are alone or going to sleep those words will keep spinning in your head. Will constantly irritate you. Unless you watch porn, masturbate, you will not get relief from the burning of thoughts.

"Little friend, how can I live without them? Do group study together, who will explain to you if you move away from them, who will get the notes from? " Satan will try to deceive you by saying these things. He listened to her words and died. These friends will destroy your life. You will be dragged to hell.

"Alas for us, if I had not accepted such a person as a friend. He misled me after the advice came to me. Satan is such a character that in time he leaves people helpless. "

(Surat al-Furqan; 25: 26-29)

"Friends will be enemies on that day, but not God-fearing."

(Surat az-Zukhruf: 43:8) Say goodbye to those friends for the sake of Allah (9). Allah (9) will make you a better friend than these In sha Allah. People cannot live alone, they cannot live in isolation. So our suggestion would be to deal with the practicing Muslim brothers ("Huzur" in the language of the society). In sha Allah their companionship will help you to overcome the addiction.

Eleven

A method of suppressing the sexual desire of the youth is known from the hadith of Rasulullah (). Fasting.256 You can start fasting two days per week, Monday and Thursday. You will see that you have come a long way in a month and a half. But Satan will not allow you to fast; "How can I fast for such a long day, there are classes, there are labs ... I can't, if I fast you will dry up, my face will be ruined ..."

Start fasting by relying on Allah (69). Allah (1) will make it easy In sha Allah. The same goes for charity. Every time you masturbate or watch porn, when you go to give alms as an expiation for your sins, Satan will warn you, "If you give alms, you will run out of money. What do you do for a month? "

These whispers cannot be given any importance. Allah (19) Himself has declared that if you give, He will increase your wealth, so do not listen to the words of Satan.

Twelve

Drama, serial, movie, song, item song, these are very terrible traps of the devil. It is not possible to take care of the eyes without being away from them. The devil can easily grab your heart to get into this trap. Needless to say, what will happen if the control of the heart is handed over to the devil. Bollywood item songs in particular are very toxic. How can a healthy normal male be stable when he sees an item song? If you can't stop watching Item Song, stop worrying about getting rid of porn-masturbation addiction. After reading so far, you must be angry with us — you can't listen to music, you can't watch movie serials, you can't make love, you can't have girlfriends, you can't chat with girls on Facebook, you can't watch random videos on YouTube ... What can be done? Is Islam so strict? There is no such thing as entertainment in Islam? What to do in retirement?

What to do in your spare time, what to watch instead of movie-serials, what to listen to instead of songs are discussed in our next article. Drop it. But before that you need to know a few things ...

America! Dreamland!

Happiness and joy float in the air of that country.

We think that being able to be like the people of that country is modernity, being able to rise, being successful in life. Whose lifestyle we blindly imitate. We have all the things we absolutely want in their lives — friends, chats, songs, reckless parties, girlfriends-boyfriends, free mixing, free sex, movies, serials, drugs ... everything. They are drowning in an ocean of entertainment. In our eyes, these Americans have everything they need to be happy in life. According to the definition of happiness that we have created, Americans are supposed to be the happiest.

But ...

But even then, why does 1 in 10 Americans suffer from severe depression?

Why do 44,193 Americans commit suicide each year? On average every day

121 people?

Why are teens in America becoming increasingly suicidal? 260

Why is the suicide rate among Americans about 24 percent higher than before? 261

Remember the final exam of a very difficult course after half an hour. There is nothing that you can do about it. The course teacher is very serious about him, he doesn't want to give numbers. And at the same time he has a past "reputation" for making it difficult to "have fun" with students. You made a PDF of the answers to some of the questions that can come in the exam helplessly and took it to your mobile. But it is forbidden to take mobile during the test. The student will be expelled from the hall as soon as he gets a mobile phone from anyone, along with a one-year drop. So in such a horrible situation, you have to gently take the mobile out of your pocket and start tuklifying the test.

Naturally you are suffering from extreme instability. Sweat has accumulated on your forehead from under the fan. Heartbeat increased. Realizing that he was scared all the time, he grabbed Sir's hand and ate it. Your mind is very restless, very restless.

Glory be to God! Just think, the peace of your mind has vanished like camphor because of breaking the laws made by the little man in the world, because of committing a very small crime. So how can you find peace in your heart when the Creator of the heavens and the earth, who created everything from non-existence, constantly breaks the law of that glorious God (19) and constantly rebels against God (4)? Tell me, how can you find peace?

God (19) told you to restrain your eyes, to take care of your eyes. "Tell the believing men to lower their gaze and guard their private parts. This is the best way for them. Surely Allah is aware of what they do.

(Surah An-Noor; 24:30)

You are constantly thumbing at his order. Swallowing with the eyes of girls in the street, doing thesis with the figure of girls with friends, the screen of your mobile turns blue in the middle of the night, surfing all the X rated websites, pornstars and item girls are your dream girl, the princess of dreams. How do you find peace?

Friends, chats, songs, GF, BF, serials, facebooking, selfies, DSLR, KFC, Pita Hat are all part of your eight hours. Thinking, quite! I am happy. Put your hand on your chest and tell me the truth, are you really at peace, are you happy? Why do you wake up one afternoon and get upset in the dead light of the last afternoon for unknown reasons? Your eyes get wet thinking about what to do in the middle of the night. The crowd gathers in the chest. The heart seems empty. What do you have! Where is an imperfection, imperfection! Where there is a lack of what! Life seems more complicated than Budd! Doesn't your mind become restless and restless when you see the waist swing and body folds of the item girls? Doesn't the animal inside the mind eat you lazily? Every time you watch a porn video, don't you want to die after masturbating? I do not think why I did, why?

What are you intoxicated brother? Intoxicated by what?

Pornstar's plump body, girlfriend's "mind blowing eyes", item girls' lascivious smiles? Do you ever find them as your own? Will not get They are nothing but mirages. They will grow old one day. The body will fold, the skin will wrinkle, the teeth will fall out, the eyes will turn gray, the hair will become like jute flax. In the end, their bodies will be eaten by insects under the ground, and the stench will spread when they rot. This is what attracts you so much! Because of these you are blowing away the fire of Hell, which will burn to the heart and whose fuel will be people and stones.

You are forgetting about your "volumetric" paradise wife who has been waiting for you for hundreds of thousands of years. Whose head scarf. Better than anything between the world and the sky. 173/234 Allah (swt) Himself is clothed about the beauty of the wives of Paradise Spending thousands of years looking in the eye - everything you can imagine, and everything you can't, will surpass the bliss of paradise. If you wish, the two of you will walk around in the garden of paradise. The fallen leaves of the tree will gently fall from the top of the head. Your wife will walk with her head on your shoulder, you will recite to her a poem of eternal love ...

Why are we throwing this infinite? What am I selling for?

Me, how crazy you are, how crazy! "... love for women, children, zodiac gold and silver, marked horses, domesticated animals and farms have been made attractive to the people. But all this is just some material enjoyment of worldly life. (But) the beauty of a lasting outcome is only with Allah. "

(Surah Al 'Imran; 3:14)

There is no peace in the glamor of fantasy, item girls in porn videos. Rather, it hurts your heart. There is no peace. In the pouring rain, sitting next to his girlfriend in the same rickshaw, he gets wet and gets wet. These can give you momentary pleasure and temporary excitement, but not peace. There is peace in obeying the command of Allah (9). There is peace in prostrating to your Lord, standing alone at night in front of the Lord and shedding tears. To enslave the Lord by disobeying one's own nafs. Believe me this peace is priceless. This peace cannot be obtained in exchange for anything in the world. Once you get this peace, you will want to get this peace again and again.

Don't give it a try. Do not take care of your eyes for a week without disobeying Allah (4) and see what the result is. Give it a try ... "... Of course, the remembrance of Allah calms the heart."

(Surah Ar-Ra'd; 13:28)

However, when autumn comes, you will be able to retire ...

I grew up with lots of light and air and a huge sky. After getting up in college, I had to move to Dhaka city full of bricks, stones, smoke and mechanics. I disliked the hostel room at first sight. Even in Bharadupura, it is very dark. There is a window, but not for ventilation; Stink and mosquitoes to enter. My soul fluttered like a bird in a cage. There is no place to sit with legs spread, no place to breathe.

I had to study day and night under the pressure of college. However, in the afternoon, even if it was a little leisure. There was nothing to do then. My life was as free as the wind, I grew up running on the field, the electronics gadget didn't bother me much, I didn't even want to read the story book after reading the class all day. I used to sit quietly in the room feeling upset. Sometimes I would walk aimlessly on the street. Rickshaw labyrinths, local buses, sidewalk peddlers, station platforms, countless isolated island-like people, trains leaving the platform with sighing whistles, the gloomy light of autumn, a small riverbank floating before my eyes.

A group of teenagers are walking in a row along the isle of mustard field. The new fog of autumn has fallen on the mustard field in absolute comfort. Stamps in the hands of teenagers, balls in someone's hands. They beat the ball on the field all afternoon. Now that's going back to whose house. The full moon of the full moon has started peeking over the ash tree.From a distant village, a calf snorted in a sad tone. Maybe calling mom. That call floated in the north wind for a long time.

When he saw the train of his city standing on the platform, he wanted to leave everything and sit on the train now.

It is very difficult to see the children of Dhaka city. What a miserable situation for them! We have created a system that sucks the vitality of children at every moment. Book loads, coaching center running and private Their life is kerosene due to the harassment of tutors. What is the benefit of putting so much pressure on them? Do not have any mercy on them. Why should he get full marks in all subjects? Why should he be like Fayaz or Farihar next door? Aren't we all different people? Each of us has a different entity, do we have some characteristics of our own? Why do we want to be the carbon copy of others?

This world would be much more beautiful if we could live our own lives without looking at the lives of others. We would not have so much tension, so much instability, mental turmoil, insomnia. Everyone could be what they wanted to be in life, what they loved. After studying engineering, he did not have to sit at the bank desk every morning with a sullen face, the boy who wrote poems in secret did not have to fight against his mind. It goes without saying that the mechanically heartless people of Dhaka city do not get full retirement after running after money, career and fame. Even then, enjoying as much as you can relax is a huge problem. How poor is the city of Dhaka! There is no sky in one chill, no place to breathe, no playground, no bamboo bush, no unadulterated moon above the head of the bamboo bush! In this way, in a chicken coop, what is meant by surviving on a table tied at nine or five?

This life is the life of cockroaches!

This life is the life of reptiles!

Yet in this city of lies filled with black and white rubbish, people dream of building a red and blue family. The mother loves her child, the wife waits for the man she loves to return home. What I started writing thinking about and how irrelevant I wrote! In many cases masturbation or porn-addiction takes on an acute form simply because leisure time is not used properly. This article will try to shed light on how to make leisure fun in spite of hundreds of limitations.

After working all day in the office or in class, hanging on the bus with a bat, a strange emptiness works inside the chest while knocking on the doorbell. This time, which means this time after returning from office or class is very delicate.

One study found that the amount of sexual arousal increases when mental stress increases or when you are anxious for any reason. 272

Those who occasionally watch porn videos or masturbate are the devil at this time

"Whatever you watch porn or masturbate, the mental stress will go away." Many respond to Satan's intrigue. Lost in the fantasy world of porn-masturbation wants to forget all the exhaustion of life. Exhaustion is gone for a moment, but after a while it comes back a hundred times stronger. Islam has not given an excellent solution to this problem! The Prophet (x) said, when the husband returns home, the wife should open the door. They exchanged greetings. The wife should dress beautifully for the husband. A wife's smiling face, a sweet-sounding salutation or two soft words, can give instant peace to a husband who is tired and devastated by all day's work, motivation to live anew, cool eyes.

"... He has created for you wives from among yourselves, so that you may have peace from them, and He has created love and kindness between you ...

(Surah Ar-Rum; 30:21)

We women have been brainwashed in the name of women's liberation in Western propaganda

I took him out of the house and brought him to the street and made him stand as an opponent of men.

The harsh, harsh environment of the workplace is taking away the tenderness and softness of women.the emptiness of the husband's mind will be removed. At the end of the day, the poor woman is returning home by herself with zero one mind. No one is getting close enough time to anyone, the distance is increasing little by little. The door is open to strangers, porn-addicts. Unmarried brothers now you may start complaining with deceitful eyes, "We don't have a wife,What will happen to us? "

Brother, marriage has become very difficult in our society. Without complaining, without suffering in the fantasy of marriage, you should try to prepare yourself for marriage. You would be wrong to think that marriage will completely eliminate your porn-addiction or masturbation addiction. Marriage can solve some, but not all. So, the fight has to start from this moment. If you are sitting for marriage, it will not work.

After returning home, you will enter the bathroom very quickly. Take a "quick" bath with cold water. The more sensitive the places, the better. In the bathroom, you should take a bath by leaving some clothes on the body without taking off the clothes completely. After bathing, you can go out of the bathroom and listen to the recitation of Quran on your mobile or sound system. You can find all the wonderful recitations of many reciters on YouTube, if you search a little. Or you can see this link: http://bit.ly/2lkMIBU. If you listen carefully, the word of Allah (1) will protect you from the deception of Satan, and at the same time help you to overcome mental stress.

"I have sent down the Qur'an which is a system of healing and mercy for the believers."

(Surah Bani Isra'il; 17:82)

At this time you will want to be relaxed by listening to music, you will not be able to listen to music at all, listen to the Quran. If you can't do it alone, you can listen to the nasheeds without music. If you search on YouTube, you will find a lot of beautiful Nasheed without music. However, it is better not to get into the habit of listening to too much Nasheed, because many times it can act as a gateway to return to listening to music. If you want to watch movie serials, you can watch Islamic lectures or documentaries. A documentary can be about nature, animals, history or any historical place. You will find many documentaries at kalamullah.com. Do not be indifferent to eye care while watching the documentary. There is no such thing as a mahram girl in Gair.

Light can take a little sleep. Can be naughty with younger siblings or little ones. These are very helpful in reducing stress. If you are away from home, in a hostel or hall, call your parents at this time. Find out. Emo, Vivar, WhatsApp, take advantage of these. Talk openly. Mental stress will go away In sha Allah. Again, the time after returning home is very delicate. Talked to a brother. Thousands of attempts are not getting rid of porn and masturbation. Stay well for a while, then watch porn for a few days in a row and masturbate. Then you stay well for a while, then porn and masturbation start again ... You couldn't get out of this loop. The brother was told to keep track of which days he was watching porn and masturbating. As it turned out, he was usually on the night before the start of the weekly holiday (Meaning Thursday night when the weekly holiday starts from Friday) Watch porn, masturbate.

In fact, the mind, overwhelmed by the stress of work all week, wants a little pleasure during the weekend, wants to get rid of mental stress, wants to "chill" a little. Listening to music, sitting on YouTube, chatting with girls in the inbox or watching movie serials to "relax" at one point, the devil is deceived and you don't even know when you go to a porn website.

I saw an army-inspired video, one after another asking in a steel-hard voice, "Who am I?" The answer from the background is in an even harder steel voice, "I am a proud soldier!"

In training, soldiers are repeatedly reminded of his identity, reminded that he is a soldier, that he cannot do anything that would insult his military identity. The word defeat should not be in his dictionary, he will never bow down, he will not retreat for a moment, his presence on the battlefield will be aggressive. Through repeated reminders, soldiers are mentally prepared to deal with the horrific situation on the battlefield.

Brother, you are also a soldier, you are constantly fighting against porn and masturbation addiction, against the devil.

When you return home, you have to remind yourself over and over again that you are a soldier, you are standing in the middle of a lot of danger on the battlefield. The enemy around you, the devil, can attack from any direction and destroy the defense tactics you have developed against porn / masturbation. I have to remind myself again and again, you are at war now. This will keep you focused. Satan cannot easily ensnare you In sha Allah.

Never stay in the room alone the night before the holiday. If you can't find anyone around, keep chatting with a good friend of yours (certainly not someone of the opposite sex). Keep updating him every ten minutes. Ask them to pray. In the joint efforts of the two, it will be possible to show the thumb to In Sha Allah Satan.

Two

One of my favorite ways to relax and unwind is to read a book. Some leisure, a mug of coffee and a good book ... Ah! What else do you want in life! Freshened up from class / work, he sat comfortably on the balcony. The gusts of wind began to blow. Fire hot tea in hand and any favorite book. Ah! Peace!

If only we could realize the power of the lifeless letters in the black ink of the book! Historically, Bengalis have never been interested in buying books, but there was a time when Bengalis borrowed books or went to the library and read a few books. Now in the age of Facebook and YouTube, Bengalis have become so bookish that it has never happened in the past. There is no alternative to reading ... Read.

What books can be read?

Very important question.

He has spent a great deal of his life reading cheap, copy-paste writers like Zafar Iqbal. Now he dies with regret. Ish! Why did I waste that time reading the nonsense marijuana writings! Books are a very powerful medium to change people's minds. If you read a couple of Himu, you will want to read Yellow Punjabi and walk barefoot all day. Of course, for those who have problems with porn / masturbation, one of the things to do is to avoid science fiction type books written with a pinch of love, a pinch of science and a pinch of marijuana. Just as these books consume time, they create a kind of wail inside your chest. Ish! If I had someone like Nira or Tithi! If only someone like Silver was waiting for me! In leisure, especially in loneliness, thousands of such thoughts will fill your head. From worry to worry, from worry to sadness, from there to frustration, and in the moment of frustration the devil will come and catch you.

So what do you read?

How many people have read the whole translation of the Quran? I have read Humayun, Sunil, Samresh's huge books, but we have not read Allah's (6) books yet. What a shame! Start reading now before the embarrassment escalates further. It is better to set aside some time for recitation of the Qur'an every day. It will last for ten to fifteen minutes. And whether you can recite it or not, read the meaning of the verses. Absolutely consistent translation from the beginning of Surah Fatiha Fall. It may seem a little uncomfortable at first, but believe me it will be a lot of fun at some point. I liked the Bengali translation of the Quran published by Al Quran Academy, London.

We have not read the biography of Rasulullah (X). You can read this too. And Rahiqul Makhtum, Sira of Ibn Hisham or Sira of

Raindrops can be read. Books like Riyadus Salehin, Hayatus Sahaba, Duniya in the eyes of the Prophet can also be read. These books are very effective in softening the heart.

Read books. Buy books. No one buys books and goes bankrupt.

Kalamullah.com is for those who don't want to spend a lot of money to buy books. Download the PDF as you wish from here. Another great way to relax is to listen to Islamic lectures. There are many channels of Islamic lectures and short reminders on YouTube. Keep subscribing to these. Try to listen to lectures regularly. These will help you to get rid of your porn / masturbation-addiction, and God (19) can change the course of your life if you want. There is a different kind of fun in listening to lectures while lying in bed fresh from work, otherwise it can't be justified. Other than that, if you listen to the lecture, you are sure to fall asleep in five to ten minutes!

Don't go in front of the TV set without going to Facebook unnecessarily on holidays and go out with your wife. I have to go to Cox's Bazar, Bandarban or outside the country, he did not say. Walk on the road next to the house, eat ice cream, eat jhalmuri, take a rickshaw around the area. Watch the moonlight together on a moonlit night, the two of you sit by the window in the dark of the house in the evening.

Two people come closer with an ocean of love through marriage. It doesn't take long for the ocean of love to dry up and turn into a dead canal. Give the wife time. Appreciate his cooking, exaggerate a little if necessary, the tide will come even in the dead canal In sha Allah.

Throughout the week, your heart is pounding at work. You are emotionally devastated. The devil conspires too much to watch porn videos. At this time you need your wife. You also need your wife. The poor thing doesn't get close to you all week. Give him some time for a day or two. Otherwise, who knows, one day you will see someone Opportunity-seeking foxes become a needle between the two of you

Come out. Alienation, divorce is not growing just like that! Let's not forget our parents when it comes to talking about "wife". Our parents did not come into the world just to earn money and cook. They also want to go out to eat, want to see Chheradwip and Nilgiri. They are human too. Take them with you. Give me time.

The unmarried will start hawking again, "We don't have a wife, what about us

Will it be? "

Play sports or do physical work when you are free. There's no point in sitting in a room like a farm chicken all day and playing FIFA, Counter Strike or Rainbow Six; If you have to play, get out of the real world and play the real game খেল play cricket, play football (it's more work). Do you live in a chicken factory in Dhaka city? No playground?

Jog on the sidewalk, break the stairs without using the elevator, walk with the rickshaw down, give a push up ওক start at ten, increase the amount of push ups three times a day — 10-13-18. Occasionally go for a swim in the pool, cycle to the office, class or tuition. The bottom line is to sweat as much as possible. Your age is such that there is a lot of energy in the body now. There is so much energy that if you don't release some energy, you will not get relief, the body knows how. If you don't release this energy in a halal way, then Iblis Bata is there to show you the haram ways. You can see that you have started masturbating to get relief, and you are watching porn videos before masturbating, whether it is softcore or hardcore or Bollywood item song.

So play sports, exercise — Release energy in a halal way. If you do physical work or sports, you will get a very solid sleep. In sha Allah, both body and mind will be strong. In sha Allah, you can also get rid of the "contradictory" thoughts that come to mind before going to sleep. A Sunnah of the Prophet (X) will also be realized if you exercise. Muhammad (pbuh) himself used to exercise regularly. He also advised others to practice horse racing, wrestling, and archery. The Prophet () said, Trap. 163

"A strong believer is better and more beloved to God than a weak believer, but there is good in everyone."

(Sahih Muslim: 6945)

So exercise, become strong by playing sports, reduce fat and become fit. Increase your value in the wedding market and blow it away

Porn / Masturbation-Addiction!

Three

There is no end to our complaints about life. Didn't get it, didn't get it. In leisure time, especially when you are alone, you are reminded of all the unaccounted for events in life. Depression and despair swallowed unknowingly. The heart is bleeding. Many times this unnecessary sadness opens the door to porn-addiction.

I'm not too old. But in the meantime I had to come back from the hospital twice. I had to read under the surgeon's knife. Indescribable pain has to be endured. I had to stay in bed for one and a half to two months. Then again and again I felt that recovery is a great blessing of Allah (19). You can walk, you can go wherever you want, you can see with your eyes, you can hear with your ears — you are drowning in an ocean of bliss. Then why so sad?

Go to the hospital occasionally at leisure with friends (of course same gender). You will see life from a new perspective. How many different types of patients! No one can see with their eyes, someone has had their legs amputated, someone is lying on a white bed preparing to go to the other side. Spirits, naphthalene, Savlon, the strong smell of drugs, the rush of nurses, the empty gaze of the relatives of the patient who came from the village to sell the land of the homestead, a different kind of cruel, ruthless world! Come back from the hospital. The mind will be softened, one will learn to be a little satisfied in life, one will learn to be grateful to Allah (1), the fear of death will arise; Which is very useful for overcoming porn / masturbation addiction.

Going to see the patient is the Sunnah of Rasulullah (). Many hadiths encourage visiting patients. The Prophet (peace and blessings of Allaah be upon him) said: If a Muslim goes in the morning to seek the care of another Muslim patient, Seventy thousand angels prayed for him throughout the day from morning to evening. And if it goes in the evening, then seventy thousand angels pray for him all night long.

(Abu Dawood: 3100; Tirmidhi: 989)

You can come back with your friends from the orphanage or old age home. These can also help in overcoming porn / masturbation-addiction. Going to the graveyard from time to time is definitely an experience that exhausts arrogance and awakens fear of God in the heart. If you haven't visited in a few days, visit once before becoming a permanent resident. Go to the graveyard and stand by the graves of your loved ones. Remember the days when they were healthy and strong. He was standing among the survivors. Imagine yourself in the place of those gravediggers. Imagine you are lying in the grave, imagine once, the moment you had fun in porn-masturbation in the world is now being repaid, your grave has been set on fire, you are wearing fire clothes brought from hell ...

Try to participate in the janaza. The mind will be soft. The heart will be towards the hereafter, you can stay away from porn / masturbation.

Four

We try to follow and imitate those who are successful in this world, who have no lack of fame, fame, money, influence and influence. Whether he is the best student in the class or the popular player, the best actor or the top rich man. How do they retire? Sitting in the corner of the house watching a movie serial, reading on YouTube, with one status after another on Facebook?

Successful people are in control of almost every single situation on the planet. Some float boats in the sea, some jump with parachutes from the sky, some climb mountains, some hike, swim, read books, cycle, spend time with family and relatives. In their spare time they learn new things — a new language, a new technology, cooking, or something else. By building up the network, Charity Raises money for the fund, volunteers in a public service organization. Try to do something productive without limiting your leisure time to just "fun" and "fun". Learn to swim, cycling, bike riding, learn to cook. Learn Microsoft Office very well, it is very important to know video editing, photo editing; Learn slowly. Learn to do a bit of programming, if you have the opportunity to do a little research on electronics. Volunteer in the mosque, you can spend time in a public service organization (there is no need if there is a possibility of free mixing of men and women).

God (9) says,

"... And those who are successful will be removed from the fire of Hell and will be admitted to Paradise. The life of this world is nothing but deception. "

(Surah Al-Imran, 3: 185)

They are the real successful people (29) who got the good news of Paradise in this dusty world. How was their retirement? How did they spend their leisure time?

The well-informed Companions of Paradise (9) used to retire in remembrance of Allah (19), in recitation of the Qur'an, in search of knowledge and in accordance with knowledge. They (9) rode horses, did archery, wrestled, practiced weightlifting, high jump, long jump. He practiced martial arts. Their (9) main focus was to establish the religion of Allah () in the land of Allah (). Try to be like them (9).

Leave the current trivial childish celebrity culture and take the best generation in the world, the generation of Quran, as your role model. Read the Qur'an, understand it, pay attention to the knowledge of the religion, clarify the concept of the basic issues of the religion like Tauhid, Al Wala Wal Bara, Millatu Ibrahim. Pay attention to your body. One thing to keep in mind is that if you are under extra pressure to do productive work in your spare time or the exhaustion of the whole week does not go away even after the weekend is over, then just relax without doing productive work in your spare time or weekend.

Your first priority will be to survive the temptation of porn / masturbation, to work productively if at the end of the day you are back in the world of porn / masturbation. Go back, then there is no need for that productive work. No pressure can be taken. Must be relaxed. Focus on your priorities. Do you want to stay away from porn / masturbation-addiction or not? If you want, you must make some sacrifices (seemingly), have no girlfriends, avoid free mixing, don't listen to music, stay away from item songs, movie serials. If you do not stay away from these traps of the devil, you will try day after day, but you will not get the expected results.

The most important thing to get out of the addiction of porn / masturbation / gossip is to have strength of mind, rely on Allah (swt) and seek help from Him. When a servant moves one hand towards Allah (9), Allah (e) moves a few hands towards him. You want to save yourself from a terrible sin, to seek refuge in the cool shade of Islam from Satan's tent. Then why doesn't Allah (69) help you? Put your trust in God. Keep asking like a stubborn person. God (4) will save you from this sin. Communicate with the mind. Listen to the heart. If you want from the heart, one day or another, the addiction to porn / masturbation / chat will have to go away.

InShaAllah

I prayed

Dua is the tool of the believer. Deadly tool. More powerful than an atomic bomb. In the power of prayer, you can defeat the hydra monster called porn / masturbation.

And your Lord said, "Call on Me, and I will answer your prayer."

I will. "

(Surat al-Mu'min: 40:60)

"Allah (e) is shy and merciful. When a person raises his hand towards him (to make du'a), he is ashamed to return it in vain. "

(Tirmidhi: 3556)

I heard a lecturer say, "If you are trying to stay away from a sinful act or bring a Sunnah of the Prophet (pbuh) into your life, but are not succeeding in it for various reasons, then you seek help from Allah (). Repent of your sins late at night.

Recite the darood of Rasulullah (SA) and pray to Allah () with a pure heart, O Allah! I want to stay away from that work but because of my nafs, because of Satan's deception I can't stay away from that sin. The environment around me is also hostile. You have full power over everything, so give me the tawfiq to stay away from that work.

Is it too hard to pray? Will it cost any time?

No. But with a little effort, a little time spent, this dua of yours will seem like an invaluable treasure to you on the Day of Judgment. Brother, seek help from Allah. | In search of open air

Then, on the Day of Judgment, at least you can say to Allah (), "O Allah! I asked you for help, I prayed to you, you forgive me now. " Pray to Allah () as if you are talking to Allah (), "O Allah! I completely surrendered to you, relying on you. You will save me from that sin or you will not catch me for that sin on the Day of Judgment. " Glory be to God! If you pray like this, you will only gain and gain. God () will either save you from that sin, or He will save you from His punishment. Your profit from both sides.

It has been narrated in Sahih Hadith that when a servant prays to Allah () and is busy with the result, he starts saying when Allah will answer my prayer, when I will get what I want, then his prayer will not be answered.

(Bukhari: 5961; Muslim: 6110)

So keep on praying to Allah () without losing hope. Yours

Dua failed

No.

In sha Allah.

"When he's addicted to porn"

While focusing on child-adolescent, adolescent-youth porn addiction, the deadly porn-addiction of married people stays out of focus. At the beginning of this book, the article titled "108 Neelpadmas" discusses in detail how terrible the addiction of married people is to porn.

Once you become addicted to porn, you can no longer find peace in your partner. Many couples force their partners to imitate pornstars in bed. Love is lost, the husband's touch in the middle of the night does not make the wife's body tremble, it seems that an animal is tearing her apart. When the storm stopped, the husband went back to sleep, while the poor wife woke up with a pair of wet eyes and full of hatred. Once the family broke up. However, with a little awareness, it is possible to control the addiction of married people to porn and its harmful effects. This article will discuss how to deal with this addiction.

If your spouse comes to you on his own and admits his addiction, then half the work of overcoming the addiction is over. All that is left is to do the rest of the work with the combined efforts of the two. But in most cases, the porn-addicted husband / wife carefully keeps the addiction secret, refusing to ask directly. As a result, the situation became more murky.

So, first we will discuss the signs of being addicted to porn.

How to understand your partner is addicted to porn:

1. Your husband will gradually become antisocial. With different family and social get-togethers he will avoid making various excuses. He will not give you the same time as before. Don't go out with you. He will not pay much attention to your values, pride and happiness.
2. Your husband's Internet addiction will go to extremes.   Stay online day and night. When he returns home from work, he will sit with his laptop or mobile. He will not have time to sit down and talk to you or any other member of the family.
3. His sleep pattern will change. You will wake up quite late in the morning due to being online all night. Sometimes it will happen that he will not stay back in bed all night, he will be online all night saying "busy with office work".
4. Delete the browser's search history.
5. Even if you are with him while walking on the road, he will want to swallow the body of other girls with his eyes completely ignoring your presence
6. Item song, music video will be excessive attraction. Don't hesitate to look at the extreme pornographic items in front of you.
7. Your husband will start to see you in a whole new way. He will be lecturing for hours on how your clothes should look and how your figure should look. You will be amazed to discover that the man to whom you were a great beauty, the princess of Amravati, the man who loved you all, loved you like crazy day and night, the man who is blaming you today Doing
8. Your husband will become like an animal during intimacy. Forcing or wanting to do something that is haraam like anal sex or heinous sex like oral sex. If you do not agree, they will scold or beat you. A lot of

times it will force you to do these things and force you despite your reluctance. Do not pay any attention to your satisfaction or dissatisfaction during intimacy, your own satisfaction will be the last word to him. The wife of a porn addict described her intimacy with her husband as follows:

"... To him I was not a man of flesh and blood, I was a commodity. He didn't fall in love with me in bed, as if only his body was present in the bed, his mind was somewhere else — maybe - or his mind was lying.

To those porn actresses — who would get aroused when she thought about it and then put the saliva on my body.. "

9) Want to keep the intimate moments of the bed on camera. 10) At one stage of porn-addiction, your husband will lose interest in intimacy with you. He is different than sharing the same bed with you

Be interested in sleeping in bed or in another room. Its a special stage of intimacy

There will be problems to be excited.

11) Your husband will violate his privacy. Only by talking to her can you understand what your husband is hiding from you. Just out of curiosity, such questions as "What do you do online at night", "What are you hiding from me", will also make your husband very angry. He will speak harshly to you, he will quarrel with you.

Experts have identified these symptoms in research on countless porn addicts. Some of the above symptoms, however, may be present in people who are strangers.

However, if you have the symptoms number 5, 6, 7, 9, 10, you can say for sure that your husband is addicted to porn. 263, 264, 265

The next step in realizing that your husband is addicted to porn is that most wives make a mistake. Some people don't pay attention at all, they think it's like that again, men can only see one or two of these, there is no problem if they see it. Some people get angry again, shout, shout at people around the world (especially when they catch their husbands in the act of watching porn). Again many wives silently shed tears, not saying anything to anyone.

In this article we will try to discuss what you should do after your husband is addicted to porn.

1) Talk to your porn-addicted husband about his porn-addiction.

This is a very important step. You have to step on this step very carefully. The situation will become very complicated if you move a little here and there.

Notice when your husband is in a good mood, then go and sit somewhere where you can talk privately, maybe in the bedroom or in a park bench. Or a secluded green sidewalk, where the two of you can walk side by side quite a distance. Keep an eye on her and tell her directly, you know about her porn-addiction, how insignificant you think of yourself because of her porn-addiction, the eight-hour flood in your heart, your body becomes disgusted with every touch of it; Tell the details.

Remind him of the first nights of marriage when the happiness of paradise came down to earth, opening the veil, keeping an eye on the first sight, seeing with all one's heart, the first touch, the first fascination with biochemical reactions. Then came the storm. The wind is blowing and your arranged family is trying to destroy you. You two have gritted your teeth, held hands and fought shoulder to shoulder, you have won. Why should you be defeated by porn addiction?

The tears of girls are very hard for men to bear. Bring tears to your eyes as you talk to your husband, remind your husband of his future if you have children. There are three possible consequences of this conversation.

i) Even before you were caught, your husband was trying to overcome his porn addiction. But he did not succeed. He will become very emotional after hearing the words in your mouth, will turn red with shame. Strictly promise to get rid of addiction.

ii) He didn't think seriously about quitting porn before he was caught. But after this conversation with you, start thinking about quitting porn addiction. Assure you that he will not watch porn anymore.

iii) Get angry when you hear. Scold you Start behaving like a stubborn Govinda. Increase the amount of porn viewing.

Your next step will depend on your husband's response. For the time being, we will think about reaction number three and think about the first two reactions.

Just as you will study the harmful effects of pornography on your own, you will also try your best to inform your husband about the dangers of pornography. You can read articles on Google, watch videos on YouTube, read books. If you can truly realize the horrors of porn addiction, a urge will come from within your husband to get rid of the addiction. At the same time, you can both get an idea of the strategies to fight porn addiction by searching the internet or books.

2) The next step is to get a counselor for yourself. The counselor can be the imam of the mosque, a trusted elderly elder close to both of them, a psychologist or a sexologist. What is the level of your husband's porn addiction, whether he has been watching porn for a while and is now in the early stages of addiction, watching softcore porn or not going without hardcore porn, for a short time or for a long time. The counselor needs to fix that. Remember, it is very important to seek the help of a counselor. There are many instances of failure to overcome porn addiction due to negligence in this one job.

3) The next step is also very important. You need to find out why your husband is watching porn videos, what is working as a trigger for your husband to watch porn. Maybe,

i) She is addicted to pornography long before marriage.

ii) After marriage, while browsing the internet, he curiously watched porn videos once or twice, then gradually became addicted.

iii) Through a friend.

iv) From erotic movies, item songs to more strict porn videos has become addicted.

v) Influenced by the surrounding sexuality-driven environment.

vi) From sexual dissatisfaction.

vii) To get rid of stress.

It is very important to identify these issues.

Never blame yourself for your husband's porn addiction. Even then, think about what happened to you that happened to you Increased your distance with your husband, created emptiness about you? And is he filling this void with porn videos?

In this sex-driven society, everything gives a man a handful of free, perverted sex. Imagine your husband working all day in the office and returning home devastated, from work co-workers to pedestrians, billboards, shop signboards, everything creates a huge void inside him. You could fill this void yourself. Two words with you, your sweet face, a smile on your sweet face, light naughtiness would fill the huge emptiness of your husband's chest with heavenly happiness. But it turned out that your husband did not find you back home, you may not be at home then, busy with your work outside the house. Or you are at home, but you did not talk sweetly to your husband, you came in front of your husband with a messy, messy look and annoyance under the pressure of housework. Or as soon as he entered the house, he started yelling, "Why didn't you bring it? How many more times? Minse, today is your day, not mine! "

The widening of the void inside your husband's chest increases a bit more. Online surfing begins. Then slowly porn-addiction. A new definition of "caring wife" has now been created for the benefit of drama-cinema. Taking care of all the issues of the husband, "Why do this, why don't you do that, why do you mix with him ..." No man wants to see a real male wife in the role of his "boss". We do not understand how many of these actions poison the minds of countless husbands, gradually create distance with the wife, start adultery, porn-addiction! Keep reminding your husband of the importance of eye care. In a joint effort, start gradually reducing movies and dramas, and at some point tell your husband to stay away from them altogether.

Retirement must be put to good use. During the holidays, spend time alone like watching movies, dramas, Facebooking, surfing YouTube. Feel how much more love is left between the two of you, put those loves in the base, go for a walk outside, walk along the sidewalk until you are tired, enjoy the rain in the rickshaw (maintains the screen). The distance that was created between you in the tension of life will be reduced A lot. Decorate beautifully for your husband. He returned home with a toxic mind after seeing exhibitions of women's bodies on the streets and at work. If you are messy, that poisonous mind becomes more poisonous, your attraction towards you decreases. As the extramarital affair begins, so does the tendency to watch porn.

How can Bengali girls grow old at the age of twenty? Keep your body fit. In the first part of the marriage, the fascination in the eyes of both of them is so intense that after a while, it is cut off by the scratch of reality. None of us admit it, but in most cases your husband's physical attraction to you will diminish as your body becomes awkwardly shaped. Love, Maya Mamata may remain the same as before, but physical attraction is definitely reduced. This empty space is occupied by alienation or porn-addiction. Make sure that your husband's physical needs are being met, and that he is getting close to you. Support your husband as much as you can during intimacy.

Keep in mind, helping your husband during intimacy does not mean that you will do it even if he tells you to have anal sex, oral sex during intimacy or to do perverted things like porn heroines. Keeping fit doesn't mean you have to be like pornstars. The problem is your husband, not you. Why would you waste your own life? You will do as much as you can within the limits of halal and haram. Nothing more.

One thing needs to be clearly understood. You are not responsible for watching your husband's porn. Whatever you do, even if you commit a crime, it does not justify your husband's porn addiction. But as a Muslim woman and wife, it is your duty to make a sincere effort to correct your husband. Those of us whose thoughts are tainted by Western feminist philosophy may not like many of our words, but these solutions are not for them. These solutions and this book speak for Muslims as Muslims, from the standpoint of Islam.

4) Set a target for your husband, "next week you will not watch porn ..." After a week, give a new target. This time for two weeks. It will continue like this. Reward him every time he can meet the target, be it for your beautifully decorated, a gift or his Cooking any food of choice; The only way to the heart is through the stomach!

5) If your husband is not able to meet the target, do not get angry with him. Give him courage, give him inspiration. I don't think women will ever understand how great a source of inspiration women are for men!

6) Your husband is sincere about ending his porn-addiction, if you understand it, give your husband time. Even if he fails again and again, be patient with him. But if you realize that your husband is not at all sincere about ending his porn-addiction, he is playing with your emotions then you have to make other arrangements. You also play with his emotions. Put a flood of tears in the book, threaten to leave the father's

house with the child, stop cooking; Hit the rice, hit the water, hit the body.

7) If you see your husband watching porn, then there is no need to say anything. It is better to stay away from him at this time. He is not in normal condition at the moment, something unexpected may happen. So talk about it sometime later.

8) It is very important to install software or apps to block porn sites on PC or phone. These websites or apps need to be installed in consultation with your husband. Not for covert espionage. Installing these without any prior discussion with your husband can be counterproductive. You will find more details on this topic in the article "**Poison poisoning**". Feel free to contact us if you have trouble installing.

9) Do not keep a working girl at home, your husband's marriage is halal with women, with whom your husband has to maintain the screen, your husband has to give advice again and again. Regularly remind your husband of the importance of the screen.

10) Do a lot of dua together. Charity must be done. We have to seek help from Allah ().

11) Keep your children away from their fathers as much as possible. Many people became acquainted with pornography because of their father's porn addiction.

12) If your husband is not sincere in his efforts to get rid of porn addiction, cheats on you again and again, and fails even after giving you a chance, then you have to think anew about your relationship. Don't make decisions alone, talk to people close to you, talk to parents. There is no need to hide anything. Then everyone has to think and decide together.

But no matter what decision you make, you must first discuss the whole matter in detail with a scholar, and you must perform the 27 prayers of Istikharah.

Let's go back to the first step. If your husband gets angry when you start talking about porn addiction, give him some time. Then say it again. Explain the horrors of porn addiction. Play with emotions, threaten to leave the father's house with the children, he will one day understand In sha Allah. Then follow the tips, starting with step 2. If you can't convince your husband in any way, if nothing works, talk to the rabbis, advice from the scholars on the next step take it.

Our children watch porn !!

First introduction

I was addicted to listening to music during class nine-ten. I used to listen to one song after another almost all the time except school and sleeping time. I couldn't know why without listening to music. At that time I had nothing of my own PC or phone. The only source to listen to music was Sony MP Five. The era of Android phone has not started yet. Nokia 2600 Classic and China phones are dominating the market. Tahsan's songs flowed from the loudspeakers of friends' China phones, I sighed and wondered when I would be the proud owner of such a "restless" phone.

Since I used to listen to songs all the time, I would get disgusted with a song in a few days. The internet was like a dream to me then. The computer shop at the corner of the street is the only hope. After a few days, I had to go to the computer shop at the corner of the street to download new songs. If he paid ten to twenty rupees, he would fill the whole MP five and give songs. Due to going to this place again and again, I got a lot of respect with the shopkeeper. So once that guy loaded my MP5 and asked for a little more money. As soon as I looked at him in surprise, he winked and said, "I gave the goods, little brother." Later I heard many similar stories from many of my friends.

Someone went to the store to download Bengali movies from Kolkata,The computer shopkeeper gave the movie as a fau he also gave some blue movies. Then slowly into her porn video addicted, he filled the cash box of the shop. Impossible too close to me a talented friend became addicted to porn videos and started studying threw. I have seen him change because of pornography from very close. This even in the age of high speed internet, I always see many computers like this load memory cards from stores (especially village and mooseballs regions). Thinking twice to buy hell for fifty-sixty rupees not these shopkeepers.

"Remember that for those who wish to spread obscenity among the believers, there is a painful punishment in this world and in the Hereafter. God knows, you don't know "

(Surah An-Noor; 24:19)

Another common way to get acquainted with porn videos is with friends who are "mature" at an early age. This group of premature friends has somehow found the porn video. Then they voluntarily take on the great responsibility of introducing the thing to their friend as soon as they see it. Share it, Bluetooth, pen drive, hard disk lenadena. The polite boy in the class wearing thick rim glasses was also forced to watch porn videos. Under the pressure of friends, he was forced to be polite, a good boy might watch porn videos once. Even if he wants to vomit at first sight, an unknown "feeling" works in his body. Wants to see again later. Then again.

In this way, even a good boy was once caught in the trap of pornography. Many times 10-12 year old boys are shocked to see the sudden changes in their body, but they cannot ask their parents about these questions out of fear or shame. Unable to satisfy his curiosity, he finally took refuge with his friends. This talk with friends, this discussion from that discussion, once the words porn, masturbation also came. In this way, many people become acquainted with porn and masturbation.

This is how many of my childhood friends got acquainted with porn and masturbation. Another way to get acquainted with porn videos is with the older siblings, cousins or older siblings (especially in the village, it is very common).

Big brother, sister or cousin is addicted to porn videos. Porn video filled with memory on his mobile or PC. Little brother, sister or cousin, he occasionally plays games on his mobile or PC. He will discover porn videos in a hurry one day. This is how a six- to seven-year-old child of a very close relative of mine came into contact with pornography. It's a pity to say that, but still, the children who are exposed to pornography through siblings or cousins are siblings There is a very good chance that those children will be sexually abused. So it needs to be taken very seriously. However, the biggest means for teenagers to get acquainted with pornography and masturbation is through the internet and satellite channels.

Forty-eight percent of teens in the United States do not search for pornography while browsing the net, but do find porn videos. (28% of 15-15-18 year olds online health content he went to Ghante and found a porn video.

In this age of information technology, you have to let your child use the internet one day or another. We are not forbidding that. But our question is, why would you put a high speed net in the hands of a child of 10-12 years? Why give them a high configuration phone? A 10-12 year old child with a high configuration phone, high speed net will do such an important job, I do not understand. Will he search the net and do research on academic studies? Download tutorial from YouTube? Will you go to Wikipedia and study? Google will search various educational topics? Will there be different educational groups on Facebook?

B. Practical! Your child will go to Google, but not to deal with "light synthesis", but to deal with porn. Do not download tutorials from YouTube, download any item with "Fire" on the newly released screen. He is rarely found in Facebook's educational groups, he is stuck in someone's rant or the time spent chatting with someone of the opposite sex.

Do you think your child is an angel? Isn't he human? Does he have any biological needs? Magazines, billboards, TV, movies, internet যৌ sexual imagery is being thrown at her from all sides. You sit in the drawing room with your child and enjoy the dancing of the Indian dancers, watching the bodies of the IPL-BPL cheerleaders Folding, watching movies, keeping Prothom Alo type magazine at home, which has faithfully fulfilled the "great duty" of introducing pornstars, dancers and prostitutes to the people of Bangladesh.

One of the items in Bollywood today is worse than an porn song. All the chemistry of men and women is being shown there. Your child is watching these, maybe sitting together with you, but you don't tell him anything. Now, if he likes an item song, he has to go around the net to download it. You have to do a Google search by typing the name of that item girl. And from these places he will find the world of pornography.

And the brave Bengali has left Google in such a state that if you type a Bengali word in Google and search, such and such scandal, rape in the dark of such and such night, the link of such news comes. Your child is in a society, in an environment where his or her biological needs are constantly being stimulated. That is in front of you, you are not taking any action, you are not taking any steps to protect your child from this sex-driven culture — he must find a way to put out the fire.

The next time an item song is played on TV, you can do a small test. Don't skip channels inadvertently like other times. Take good care. Try to see each frame of the video through the eyes of a 10-12 year old boy or girl. Listen carefully to the lyrics. Dozens or hundreds of such items will try to think calmly about what kind of impact a 10-12 year old or younger boy or girl can have on the thinking and behavior in today's society and culture. I hope it will not be difficult to understand the truth. These items continue to create porn addiction.

Children are exposed to pornography at the age of 10-12, and children are secretly watching it. But you yourself are leaving the TV all day, leaving Bollywood songs while feeding, introducing the very young child to item addiction, where in many cases the chemistry of men and women is being shown more provocatively than pornography. Sometimes he leaves a "hit" song in the market and says to him, "Babu! Show me a little dance "or" Babu listen to a little song ". Have you ever wondered how much you are destroying him with your own hands?

How to understand your child is addicted to porn:

1) After watching porn, usually the history of the browser is deleted. If you notice that your child is deleting browsing history, you know he's doing something online that he doesn't want anyone else to see. Maybe she is making love online or watching porn videos. The latter is more likely to

happen. According to a 2012 survey by Tru Research, 71 percent of 13- to 16-year-olds delete their browsers or chat history so their parents have no idea what they're doing online.

By 260 2) Up children will be very picky about privacy. Keep the door closed. Own house

3) He will be shocked if you enter the house in a hurry. Notice the unusual movement in him. He will minimize the tab quickly. Will be staring at the desktop wallpaper. Keep your hand on the mouse and keep clicking here and there, refreshing the page.

"What are you doing?" When asked, he would smile shyly, this is what he said will try or get angry.

4) Will use mobile while hiding under kantha / blanket.

5) Will use mobile at night. Sitting in the corner of the room all day on the PC rather than hanging out or playing.

It will be very quiet. He will sit next to you for hours looking at the screen, will not move, will not say anything. You will notice the abnormality in his appearance. For example: the face will turn red, you will breathe loudly.

6) Take the mobile to the bathroom. Will spend longer in the bathroom than before.

7) Turn the PC screen towards the wall, so that what is going on the screen can not be seen.

8) When you visit a porn site, the amount of popups usually increases. While browsing the net you will catch a lot of popup notifications suffering from pain, Dalme Kuch Kala Hai.

9) He will show unusual curiosity towards sex. You may even face unwanted questions.

10) In his behavior, gestures will have the impression of imitating pornstars.

11) You will discover he is masturbating.

If you have these symptoms, you will understand that your child is watching porn. Of course, some of these (2, 4) also indicate that your child has a "mind" transaction with someone else. 261, 272, 273

Way now?

One morning you discovered that your child was watching pornography. Severe trauma. The innocent holy face of your child floated before your eyes. You didn't understand how a piece of your body became addicted to this heinous drug and you didn't even notice. What do you do now? Snatch laptop-PC? Do you quarrel with two slaps? Will you take him out of the house by the neck, or will you marry him? How to get the child back from the dark world of blue? How do you talk about this embarrassing thing?

We will discuss some possible solutions to these complex problems, In sha Allah.

1) Do not panic at first.

The mistake that most parents make is to hold their child in their arms while watching porn or if the child is watching porn in some way, then they lose their senses in anger. Never make this mistake. Give your child a chance to talk openly with you. When you get angry,The next time you may be doing a lot of things behind your eyes that you will never know. Please don't say "this is my son's fate", "I have taught you this", "don't show your face in front of me". Be a little patient.

Believe me, once your child is convicted, a kind of guilt will work in your child. This shame is enough for him. Do not embarrass him with unreasonable threats. Remember that sexual curiosity is not uncommon. We all have an interest in sex and sexuality. This is our innate fitrat. You haven't talked to your child about these things on your own or he or she has had a communication gap with you, as well as the sexual-driven environment around him or her.

Your child is just an innocent victim of pornography. Your child maybe on his mobile or attracted to the persuasion of his friends or someone else inspired to watch pornography on laptops. The way the internet is the market for pornography It is difficult to escape from its destructive and toxic outbreak stands. Other than that, the websites that do not have anything obscene advertisements are also often drawn to pornography. So again, please don't be angry. At first maybe your son or may be a pity for the girl. But still the child with enough empathy talk to Explain to him, "Look, Dad, I'm sorry that you saw them. Believe me, I'm not angry with you. My anger is on them who have spread such things among you. "

Explain to your child that sex is not a dirty thing. Children need to be told the realities of sex. And who can tell them better than you? Don't be ashamed! As children get older, curiosity about sex will grow. If you don't have a moderate discussion with your child about sex that goes with their age, he or she will go to someone else to satisfy his or her curiosity. That could be friends, cousins, the internet. And this is where porn-addiction can start. At the same time, there is a risk of being sexually harassed. Never rely on school for your child's sex education. Also, keep a close eye on what your child is being taught in a sex education course from school, and look at his / her books from time to time.

There is a terrible conspiracy going on all over the world about sex education. Children are being attracted to perverted and forbidden sex in the name of sex education. Kindergarten children are also not being exempted. Five-year-olds in Germany are being taught how to use condoms, how to reach orgasm! In the name of 264 sex education, Dr. has done remarkable research work on how the lives of millions of innocent children around the world are being destroyed. Judith Riesman, however, is not coming up in the media to go against the agenda of sexualizing the society. We will specifically request. To watch the video below from Judith Ryman's website,

Explain to your child that sex is a gift from God to us (9), the right of which is to be achieved through marriage. This is the way to keep the lineage alive on earth. Through this we are able to establish a strong and intimate relationship with our spouse. This is a plan prescribed by Allah (19) to maintain the balance of the family. Sex is not to awaken one's own animality. If your 8-10 year old child has fallen into the trap of pornography, explain it to him or her.

"Look, I know you were shocked at first by what you saw, you didn't enjoy it at all. That's normal for a boy or girl your age. You are not old enough to adapt to all this. Did you know that our Creator created this system for us? But it is only for mothers and fathers who can do it only through marriage. This is a very secret matter. God (69) never commanded it to be beaten. He does not like such work at all. Everything has its ups and downs. The same goes for sex. This kind of filth about sex makes our creator angry.

Look, your eyes are not being guarded by what you see. But Allah (swt) has commanded us in the Qur'an to take care of sight and place of shame To do. He will love you very much if you follow his word. He will admit you to a paradise where you can do whatever your mind desires. You don't have to do homework there, you don't have to go to school. You can do whatever you want to do there as soon as you want it. And if you disobey Allah (19) and see all this, Allah (84) will punish you in the fire of Hell. There is only pain and suffering. Now tell me which one do you want? "

If your child is a little older, explain it to him or her, but try to keep the tone of the speech.

2) The next step is to teach your child the horrors of pornography. It is very, very important. If he doesn't have a clear idea about the harmful aspects of pornography, then today or tomorrow he will start watching porn videos.

In 2010, North London Secondary School's 14-18 year olds were surveyed. It is estimated that 30 percent of people have viewed pornography online since the age of 10. Eighty-five percent said their parents had never talked to them about watching pornography. 265 Discuss in detail with your child. What will come up in your discussion or how you will present it will depend on the age of your child. You should not be ashamed to talk to your child. If you are helpless, you can read books to your child about the horrors of pornography, you can show videos. But make sure he gets a clear idea of the horrors of pornography.

3) Start motivating your child to get rid of porn addiction. Ask them to follow the tips in this book.

4) Do not let your child be alone, especially in lazy times. Because, lazy time is one of the reasons for being addicted to pornography.

Keep him engaged in various sports or productive activities. Keep away from video games as much as you can. Popups of online video games often search for porn sites. Take him on a family trip once a week if you can. Give him time.

Our eyes are dazzled by the glamor of the Firingis' senseless civilization. We have made being like them the absolute vow of our lives. We don't have the opportunity to give time to our family day and night in pursuit of money, status and career. Even compassionate mothers nowadays have come to work in the office-court outside the home in the false hope of forgetting the heartbreaking cries of their children. The child is the man to the boy. Parents are filling the gap by depriving the child of affection, caress and love for the sake of career, with electronic gadgets, toys, expensive clothes and a sky of freedom. That freedom is making children imprisoned in brick-wood-stone cages addicted to porn or addicted to drugs.

I burned my mother a lot for eating rice as a child. Mother has eaten rice with so much effort, patience, listening to Dalim Kumar's story, showing squirrels and bulbuls behind guava leaves. Such stories belong to almost every child of our generation.

The working mothers of the age deprive their children of their love and affection all day long, even if they return home at the end of the day, the story does not change much. Maybe your baby is waiting for you all day long. But you can't give him time for too long in a tired body. If you don't want to eat rice, put it in front of the cartoon. You rest by holding the electronic gadget in the child's hand. Gradually a wound began to form in his small mind. Gadget-addiction makes him porn-addicted.

Sit still and think coldly. Why are you working so hard day and night? Why are you running after money? Is it money to survive, or money to survive? If you can't give your child time, can't make your child human, then what will you do with so much money, career? Sister, what will you do if you become independent, financially self-sufficient, if a part of your body spends its whole life arrogantly hating you, hating you?

Notice who he is mixing with, where he is going. Teach him how to technically say "no" if a friend or someone else insists on watching porn. Talk to your cousins and find out what they're talking about. Make him accustomed to screening and guarding his eyes from an early age. Encourage the opposite sex to screen with cousins or friends.

Many parents do not take it seriously. People think they are like their siblings, little people without them ... what's the problem?

Believe it or not, porn addiction can lead to horrible sins like adultery. There are many examples. Mami, aunty, you also have to make sure that she can adhere to the veil with the mahrams in this type of ghair. You also have to be careful about the working girl. If you want to stay at someone else's house at night often, you have to check what is the matter. Her bed has to be separated. He will not share the bed with anyone else.

Many of these may seem exaggerated to you. But the reality is completely different. It is unknown at this time what he will do after leaving the post.

5) Introduce him to the heroes of Muslim history. Keep trying to take Rasulullah (3) Sahaba (9), Salaf, Sultan Nur ud-Din Jangi, Salah ud-Din Ayubi, Tariq bin Ziad, Muhammad bin Qasim as role models. If your child's role model is Bollywood, Hollywood's characterless hero-heroine or a sports personality, then rest assured that day by day he will be morally degraded, will form friendships with porn videos. Even if you want to come back from porn addiction, you can't come back easily.

6) Do not keep anything at home that leads to pornography. Prothom Alo's "Naksha", "Adhuna", "Kishore Alo", "Ananda" or the daily entertainment page, Sananda, Anandalok or any such magazine. Item songs, music videos, Bollywood and Hollywood movies — these can also cause your child to become addicted to pornography.

7) Remove the PC or laptop that you are letting your child use at home, in the drawing room or in a room where everyone's eyes will fall at least once.

8) Decide how much time your child will spend on the Internet.

9) Encourage your child to observe Nafl fast on Mondays and Thursdays. This is the method given by Rasulullah (X) to control sexual instinct.

10) If you want you can arrange marriage for the child. Marriage porn / masturbation addiction is not a complete solution, we have already discussed this. However to reduce

the level of addiction and to become addicted to those who are not yet addicted can save from marriage.

11) Pray a lot. Give alms.

12) Use software or apps to block porn websites. You will find a detailed discussion on this in the article titled "Poison poisoning".

13) Give your child some time to get rid of porn addiction. He can't stop watching porn in a hurry. It will take time. Do not get angry even if you hold her by the hand while watching porn during the treatment. Above all, we have to rely on Allah (). Dua to Allah () lots to do.

Poisoning

It is very important to install software or apps to block porn websites to get rid of porn addiction. It is difficult to get out of porn addiction if you want to watch porn, high speed internet in the palm of your hand, two clicks, then a huge collection of porn videos. In this article, we will look for some of the software and apps that will help you get the logistics to deal with online fitnah.

K9 software

Of all the porn blocking software, K9 Web Protection is our most preferred. The K9 software works well. Just by installing this software, you can make your PC impenetrable for accessing porn sites. In sha Allah!

K9 Software Installation Tutorial - http://bit.ly/2FCWxl3 Download K9 Software From Here - http://bit.ly/11gZmes

You can find PDF tutorial on installing K9 software here -

http://bit.ly/2CvZ8LA

Blocking porn sites on Android phones

One of the most popular porn sites, Women and Tech, says that 72% of their visitors use mobile phones to browse their sites. Juniper research conducted in 2016 shows that about 250 million people have watched porn videos using mobile phones or tablets. Compared to 2013, which is about 30 percent more With the improvement, the amount of porn viewing using smartphones has increased. You have to have a mobile phone, it is not so important to have a laptop or PC, again mobile phones are cheap. Being much smaller in size than a laptop or PC, it can be taken anywhere, in the bathroom, under the canopy, behind the curtains, pressed everywhere. So it goes without saying that mobile phones will be at the top of the list of porn addicts' choice as a means of watching porn. Smart phones are also a possible means for children to become addicted to porn. It is very important to take the help of internet filtering system to keep people of all ages from children and teenagers away from the dark world of porn.

There is a great software called K9 to block porn sites on PC. But the sad thing is that most porn sites are browsed with a mobile phone, there are no good apps to block porn sites on that mobile phone. The ones that are there are also not self-contained or free. You have to buy with money. Money is not a big deal, the big thing is the complexity of buying apps online as well as the apps not being self-sufficient. Due to this complication, porn blocking apps are no longer installed on smartphones.

Brothers who are good at making apps will be requested to think about this. Pay close attention to the fact that it is very necessary but neglected to use the qualifications that Allah (4) has given you. The entire Muslim Ummah and mankind is looking at you. Rely on Allah (19) and start working, Allah () will make it easy In sha Allah.

Let's discuss how to block porn sites on Android phones with patchwork:

(1) Open DNS by changing the address

If you use the internet only with WiFi, you can block porn sites in this way. If you use the internet with mobile data, porn sites cannot be blocked using this method. Video tutorial - http://bit.ly/2mwVkD5

2) Through the spin browser

This is our preferred method. Quite effective. Download the necessary apps from the Play Store,

Spin Browser - http://bit.ly/2cJ5uf App Lock - http://bit.ly/1jjyav2

Video Tutorial - http: //bit.ly2FICLI

Protect from the temptation of YouTube

We have already discussed the fitnah of YouTube. Install K9 software for PC. Another great way to protect yourself from pornographic or sexually explicit videos on YouTube is to keep the suggested video list free of pornography. The videos that YouTube shows in your suggestion list are basically based on a few things. They want you to serve the kind of video you like. And that's why if you watch different Islamic videos over and over again, they start showing such videos in the sidebar on the right. The same goes for pornographic videos.

Second, videos from the numerous YouTube channels you subscribe to will continue to show you. Now if the channels you subscribe to are all Islamic channels, then pornographic videos will not get a chance to come in front of you. This method is very effective. You can keep your YouTube environment sacred. To subscribe, you must first sign in (log in) to YouTube. And for this you have to have a Gmail ID.

After going to YouTube, you will see "Sign In" written in the right hand corner. After clicking on "Sign In" and logging in with your mail ID, subscribe to their channels with various Islamic video searches. You can do ten or twelve at a time so that other pornographic videos do not find a place in the suggestion list. In addition, if you go to http://viewpure.com and paste the link of a video to access the video, no suggestion list will come, In sha Allah. You can be safe from pornography at least a little bit. The following two videos discuss how to avoid the temptation of YouTube on Android phones. Don't forget to check it out.

1)http://bit.ly/2FzKipk

2) http://bit.ly/2mzHpfz

Necessary apps download link:

Youtube- http://bit.ly/2cqx4QM

App Lock- http://bit.ly/1jjyav

Unsolicited ad block

Unsolicited ads online can cause terrible problems. Apart from that, these unwanted ads reduce the browsing speed a lot. You can use Adblock as an add-on to remove unwanted online ads. Available for both Firefox and Chrome.

(1) Adblock for Google Chrome - http://bit.ly/1bia3G6

2) Adblock for Firefox - https://mzl.la/2C198om

Download these two apps for Android phones:

AppBrain Ad Detector- http://bit.ly/2dhkPTo

Free Adblocker Browser- http://bit.ly/1PGjcNY

To know step by step how to download and install, watch the video tutorial below - http://bit.ly/2CHMJrk You can also block porn site by changing the address of the WiFi router.

We request readers on our YouTube channel (Lost Modesty -

http://bit.ly/2Dg7eLR) to keep a regular eye.

Who, how to use?

1) If you are addicted to porn, install these apps / softwares with the help of a close friend. Only your friend will know the password, no one else. Even if you want to, you can't break the protection and watch porn online.

2) If your husband is addicted to porn, discuss with him and install the apps / software. Only you will know the password.
3) You protect your child from online pornography

Install apps / software. Your child's password in any way Don't let me know. It is better to have an open discussion with him before installing apps / software.

Along with installing software / apps, you should also try to increase the fear of Allah (19) in your heart. In fact, it is more important than anything else. If there is fear of Allah (i) in one's mind, if there is goodwill, then porn-addiction can be overcome without any other way In sha Allah. But if the disease in the heart is not removed, no matter how many apps-software or tips you use, you will slip away at some point or another. Wama Tawfiqi Illa Billah.

I will spread the stars

One.

You know, friend, I've committed a serious sin tomorrow. There was no one in the room,

Close the door, go online ...

Stop, brother! Don't talk anymore.

The sin that Allah () has not been noticed by anyone other than Allah (), the sin that Allah () has kept hidden from man, if you know what you are destroying yourself by revealing it in front of everyone, you will tear your hair one by one. He would have become, but he did not regret it.

The Prophet (s) said, "All my ummah will be forgiven, except the one who reveals. And surely it is a great presumption that a person commits a crime at night which Allah () has concealed. But at dawn he began to say, O so-and-so! I did that tonight. But he spent the night in such a state that Allah () hid his deeds, and he got up in the morning and opened the veil of Allah () over him. "

(Sahih Bukhari: 5721)

According to another narration, Allah () will tell the angels on the Day of Judgment to go and call such and such a servant of mine. The angels will come with the servants and make them stand before Allah (). Allah () will say to His servants, O my servant! Come to me The servant will come and stand near Allah (), Allah () will call the servant closer. Servant God () will stand closer. In this way the servant will get so close to

Allah () that he will be covered by the light. God () and there will be only a curtain between them. No angel can see him, nor can he hear him Allah ()And slave conversation. Only Allah (9) and His servants. Allah (69) will say to His servant, "O Abdi, look at your record, see for yourself how you came to earth."

The servant will look at his record — only sin and sin, sin after sin.

Allah () will say, "O Abdi, do you not know that you are secretly working?"

Do I see that too? Don't you know that one day you will be mine

Stand in front? Don't you know that one day I will do all your work?

Ask about it?

The servant will answer, "O Rabb! I knew, I knew ... I knew.

Allah () will say, then why did you do these things? The servant will answer, O Rabb! It is much easier for you to throw me into hell than to judge me by standing in front of you with the burden of this sin.

Allah () will say, turn the page, go to the next page.

The servant will go to the next page and see the whole thing with more heinous sins than before

Full. In this way he will look at the pages of the whole diary. On each page he will see more, more heinous sins than the previous page. The servant will be very upset. Disappointed, he will think that Allah () will surely throw me into the pit of

Hell now. I did good deeds, but where did they come in handy? My sin destroyed me!

God () will say to the servant, O Eternal! Why did you hide your sins in this world?

The servant will answer, O Rabb! I was ashamed of my sins.

Allah () will say, "Have you not seen that I have hidden your sins from man on earth?" It was my mercy to you. Even today I will keep your sins hidden from people.

(According to another narration, Allah () will say, "In the world, you should hide the faults of your Muslim brother, so today I will also hide your faults.") Allah () will tell the servant, now turn the page of the record.

As soon as the record is opened, the servant's eyes will rise to his forehead. Just good work throughout the whole diary. There is no sign of sins. Even the angels will not know that Allah (19) has removed all the sins of His servants from the record and filled them with good deeds. Then the servant will be forgiven .

My brother, if you can't stop watching porn videos or masturbating, try to keep these hidden from everyone, there is no sin except Allah () do not keep witnesses. If Allah (e) has mercy, He may be your secret keep the sins hidden in the world and on the Day of Judgment forgive you. Why get out of telling everyone unnecessarily lose the opportunity? Sitting together with friends watching porn, girls figure who with friends just to have fun analyzing or for no reason how many porn views, how many gigabyte collections, who masturbates how many times don't hit the ax on your own feet by discussing these, brother.

One day you will have to regret to do all these "fun". But then nothing to do there won't be.

Two.

A few years ago, a multilevel business company called "Destiny" made a lot of noise in our country. Although they were thieves, the concept of multilevel marketing was great. You will get some commission from the income of each of the people you join in their company. If too many people join their company through you, then one day it will be like that, without doing anything, you will easily earn a couple of lakhs of rupees a month. Sit down and just eat with your feet on the floor and sleep with oil on your nose.

Subhanallah, in the business of trading the paradise of the servant with Allah () the sin and virtue of the servant is calculated in this way. Think, through you God guided someone. Then some thawab will be added to your thawab account from the person who will do good deeds (the person doing the deed will also get the full thawab of his amal. The reward of his share will not decrease at all). Again, if a person commits a sin because of you, disobeys Allah (19), then that person will be punished for that sin and you will have to share the punishment with him. Such a description has come in the hadith.

"... If a person calls in a good way, he will receive the same reward as all the people who follow him, but there will be no shortage of rewards for those who follow him. And if a person calls to a delusion, he will get the same amount of sin as all the people who follow him, but there will be no shortage of sins for those who follow him. "

(Sahih Muslim: 6960)

Allah () has clearly forbidden us in the Qur'an not to help one another in sin. Allah (swt) says: "... You shall help one another in righteousness and piety. Sin and

They will not help each other in transgression. "

(Surah Maidah; 5: 5)

My brother, think a little about your own lifestyle and see how you are disobeying Allah (s) step by step. Spreading obscenity among friends knowingly or unknowingly. Inducing friends with hard disk porn videos, sharing links to porn videos with them, poisoning their minds with juicy discussions about item girls, class girls.

Put your hand on your chest and ask yourself a question today. What good is a web site if it simply "blends in" with everything else out there? Seriously, what is your benefit? When you see these forbidden things, you are committing a great sin, but you are also getting "primitive" fun. But what do you gain by watching your supplied porn videos when your friends are satisfying their cravings?

There is no profit.

But you also have to shoulder the burden of your friend's sins. The more you share your porn videos or item songs with your friends and the more fun it is to watch them, the more your sins will be added to your account. You have nothing but fun, but on the Day of Judgment you will be seen as the master of sin. How do you feel then? Isn't that madness? Do not kill the ax on your own feet?

Imagine for a second you were transposed into the karmic driven world of Earl. What will happen to you then? Even if you go to the grave, you will continue to earn sins. Is there any point in doing such madness? The life of the world is one, isn't it? Does it make any sense to gamble? You can't stop watching porn videos yourself, you can't take care of your eyes. See for yourself, have fun and keep committing sins at your own risk. But don't forget to do something that will spread obscenity among your friends and the people around you. Be very careful! Pornography may spread among the people on your friend list through a click or comment you make on a Facebook post or a link you share. We also need to be careful about these matters.

Many girls post pictures of themselves on Facebook. You may upload these pictures without thinking about it, but these pictures of yours are a small ember, which can grow big and burn a huge forest at once. You have to be a partaker of the sins of those who fall into temptation by looking at your pictures, those who fall into sin. What do you need with pictures on Facebook? What do you need sister?

"Remember those who wish to spread obscenity among the believers for there is a painful punishment in this world and in the Hereafter. God knows, you don't know.

(Surah An-Noor: 24:19)

Not a fairy tale!

Extreme winter night. The cold wind is piercing the clothes and shaking the bones. A beautiful young woman moved forward in a strong, quick step and shook the door of a lonely house. A young man opened the door and saw the beautiful young woman in front of his eyes and immediately closed the door.

The girl shouted from the street, "Please let me enter your house. I'm out on tour. I thought I would be able to reach my destination before nightfall. But it's night and I'm still in the middle, I don't know where I came from. I don't know anyone in this area. If you don't give me shelter in your house, I'm afraid something bad could happen to me if I'm outside. "

"There are many more houses nearby ... please go to one of them, in sha Allah they will help you." The young man replied. The girl left. Actually pretended to leave. On a bone-chilling winter night, the girl's hard move in that lonely house, asking for shelter for a visit are all part of a heinous plan. To understand the plan, we need to know the events behind it.

This young man was a pious servant of Allah (). He used to fast all day and stand in Nafl Salat all night and shed tears for fear of Allah (). He carefully protected himself from all kinds of haraam. His neighbors did not have much of an advantage. Haram-halal did not care. They spent their days gossiping, gossiping, gossiping and slandering. The young man did not have much contact with the neighbors. Most of the time he would sit in his own house and worship Allah (). The neighbors became very angry. They used to criticize this young man all the time, "Look, look at this batter! We don't care, aren't we human? Sitting at home all day and chanting tasbih, he does not associate with us. Let's teach the boy the virtue of being born. "

Everyone conspired to overthrow this young man. Glory be to God! Satan does not always attack people directly. He sometimes forms a group of people who try to divert other people from the path of Allah ().

The young man's neighbors searched the surrounding area in search of cows, looking for a beautiful, lascivious girl. They found a young woman who was the most beautiful in the area. The people suggested to the girl, "We want you to trap the young man in such and such an area and make him stumble ... to commit adultery with him."

"Oh God! I am a girl, how can I do such a thing? "

"You make us do this. You can't imagine what you will get in return. You will be given gold equal to or more than your weight. Agree? "

The girl thought for a while. It can be said that he fought with conscience. He was very poor. Panta furaya condition to bring salt. So many resources in one push. This is not a bad thing to do. Only once! He understood himself.

"All right. When you say so much. I agree. "

.... Hearing the young man's words, the girl pretended to leave. After a while he knocked on the door again. "I went to the houses next door but none of them were at home. It is very cold outside. I'm so scared, if you don't let me in your house I might die in the cold! Please open the door. "The plea fell on the girl's voice.

"If you go down a little further down the hill, you will find some more houses there. In sha Allah they will let you stay with them. Only me in my house, no one else. It would not be right for the two of us to be together. " The young man's simple confession. The girl left. After a while he came back again. There was a knock on the door. Again the young man opened the door and saw the girl. The girl said, "By God! If you do not allow me to enter and if a man snatches my honor, I swear by Allah! On the Day of Judgment, I will stand before God and say that you are the one who caused this. I was raped because of you. "

When the young man heard the name of Allah (4), his soul trembled, because when the name of Allah (19) is remembered in front of the believers, their hearts tremble. The young man opened the door and moved away.

"Come on, you spend the night in this room, I'm staying in the next room. Please

Don't bother me anymore and it's mine as soon as it's time for Fajr

You will leave home. " Having said that, the young man went to the next room. He did not make the mistake of closing the door of his house aloud before starting the recitation of the Qur'an. The young man's neighbors were lurking nearby. As soon as the girl entered the house, they looked at each other and started laughing: "Batter sadhugiri will end soon." They want to sit like this for a while longer. Then, at the very last moment, he plans to attack the young man's house and catch the young man and the girl in handcuffs.

The young man was reciting the Qur'an with a concentrated mind. Suddenly a blood-curdling scream came from the girl's house. The young man entered the room with a lamp in his hand. The sight in front of his eyes made him a mere statue.

The girl is lying in bed. There is not even a thread on the body. Intense desire in both eyes.

The young man saw for the first time in his life something he had never seen before. He began to feel the existence of something inside him that he had never felt before. His mind told him to do something he had never said before. The most beautiful girl in their region is now in front of him. Inviting you to get lost in the forbidden world! What will he do?

What does a young man do in this situation?

The locals had already surrounded the house. This time they shortened their circle and stood close to the wall of the house. And after a couple of minutes they will break down the door and enter the house. After the young man entered the girl's house, the girl's screaming stopped.

The silence of the state descended for a while.

In the distance a nocturnal bird flew from one tree to another.

A bunch of snow fell from the leaves of the tree.

Suddenly a blood-curdling scream came from the young man's house, again. The girl's throat. She is screaming. It is doing, there is no smell to stop.

The locals knocked on the door without a moment's delay. Then the girl and the young man discovered both on the floor of the same room!

The girl had trapped the young man in the trap of her appearance. The young man was walking towards her with one foot and two feet to respond to the call of the girl. But even in this delicate moment, the young man did not forget about his Lord, the punishment of the Lord. After taking a step towards the girl, he was holding his hand over the fire of the lamp and reminding himself, "Remember, the fire of hell is hotter than this fire of the world." She was lying on the floor in intense pain. Again he was standing up. He was taking another step towards the girl ... and whenever he started moving towards the girl, he was pushing his hand into the fire and reminding himself, "Remember, the fire of hell is more intense than the fire of the world."

The girl could not bear this incredible scene. His first scream was part of the plan. But next time it was remorseful, scary.

After removing the girl from the house, the young man, burning with remorse, returned to Allah (swt): "O Allah! Forgive me for the sins I have committed. "

What was that sin? What did he do?

She refrained from committing adultery, she is the most beautiful girl in the area

Refrained from approaching, did he commit any sin at all! But he said, O God! Forgive me for those steps I took towards the girl. |

I sat in silence for a while after hearing this incident. Imagine for a second you were transposed into the karmic driven world of Earl. Your young body, your togbag blood, a beautiful woman has voluntarily surrendered to you behind the black sheet of the night. No one is anywhere. What will you do when the crows will not notice anything? What is normal to do? There is nothing to be surprised about having a heart attack with joy.

What do we think when we get home empty or get room alone?

This is the opportunity to watch porn or masturbate! Isn't it?

Let's be honest.

No one was home or the room was empty and we didn't watch porn videos, masturbate or indulge in sex fantasies with any girl.

Has that happened? What happened once?

What will be our courage to speak the truth with our hands on our chests?

Glory be to God! The roots of this boy's faith are deeply rooted. His faith did not waver in the storm of forbidden love that the beautiful young woman raised in the middle of the night.

Alas! How weak is our faith!

Pornstars who can't be touched in an unreal world in a lonely room, our faith becomes wind as soon as we think about it. It is not too late for us to login to the net to watch porn and masturbate. In the park, under the hood of the rickshaw, in the back seat of the bus, in the elevator — we find solitude, in the crowd of local buses, we find opportunities in concerts. Playing "Just Friend-Just Friend", "Sibling" games all day, cooling ourselves in the bathroom late at night. We have sinned so much that we no longer think of sin as sin. We don't feel bad after masturbating or watching porn. It doesn't matter to us. An integral part of life.

This young man was a man of flesh and blood just like us. He also had a heart like ours, he had desires in his heart, he had an incomprehensible attraction towards women. But he did not bow to that desire. He is also a servant of Allah (19), we are also a servant of Allah (1), but our heaven and hell are different from him. Sitting in the shadow of the Throne of Allah (19) on the Day of Judgment and drinking Kausar's drink, we may be humiliated for our sins committed in the dark of night.

I heard about a boy in the mouth of a Shaykh who used to remember Allah (69) more than 12,000 times a day. He was asked, "Why do you remember Allah so many times?"

He replied, "May I defeat Abu Hurairah (4). Abu

I can remember Allah (4) more than Hurairah (9). If she can ignore the Danakata fairy, then why can't we stop watching little porn videos and stop masturbating?

My brother ...

My brother, you man is very valuable. A drop of tears from your repentant heart is very, very dear to the owner of this universe. For you, the most beautiful man in the world would spend sleepless nights and pray to his Lord. 1400 years ago that man (*) loved you so much that he (3) prayed to Allah (69) for six consecutive hours in the hot summer sun on the plain of Arafat that Allah (9) may forgive you, you will be in Paradise, your original home. Lets go back.

The Prophet (peace and blessings of Allaah be upon him) said, "If someone assures me of two things, then I assure him of Paradise. Those two things are the tongue and the place of shame between the two runs. "

(Bukhari: 6109)

My brother, the man (Å) who was wounded by a stone in Taif for you, lost his teeth on the plain of Uhud, whose life's thoughts were all around you, you will meet him (Å) when you meet him on the Day of Judgment. What would you answer? Which face will you go in front of him?

My brother, once you imagine, you are browsing various porn websites, swallowing Bollywood item songs, how embarrassed would you be if your mother, your father saw you in such a situation? What will happen to you if the angel of death comes in front of you? When you are raised in this state on the Day of Judgment, when your hands, your feet, your eyes testify against you, the door of the room closes, what you did alone in the middle of the night will be revealed to a billion people, you will be ashamed. Would like to merge with.

Think about that day.

"Happiness from haraam ends soon

All that remains is shame and disgrace

At the end of the day there is only emptiness and the burden of sin.

The end result of the punishment of hell fire?"

THE END

Made in the USA
Las Vegas, NV
29 May 2022

49520760R00138